Praise for *The Secrets They Kept*

"Ms. Handler has written an important book about a decades-old family secret: an aunt diagnosed with Schizophrenia and her anguished father, the parent who took his own child's life rather than commit her to an insane asylum. Whereas most authors only focus on the story, Ms. Handler attempts to collate important medical, legal and societal concepts related to this tragic event. *The Secrets They Kept* is a valuable guide to further understanding the broad-reaching scope of a very serious mental condition. Ms. Handler is an excellent teacher with an insatiable thirst for understanding the human condition. Do not miss this read!"

Howard Fisher, M.D., Psychiatrist, Colorado Mental Health Institute at Pueblo

"This beautifully written book illustrates what family therapists have long known: well-kept secrets in families often have a long-ranging impact on the emotional lives and the relationships of its members for generations. There is tremendous shame and guilt perpetuated in families as a result of secrecy, perhaps more so when it concerns mental illness. Ms. Handler's careful research and efforts to unravel the silence within her family provide the reader with an informative backdrop as to the treatment of mental illness in this country during the first half of the twentieth century."

Bonnie Mucklow is a licensed professional counselor, licensed marriage & family therapist, and Level III addictions counselor. In addition, she serves as a military family life consultant for the Department of Defense and is past president of the Colorado Association for Marriage and Family Therapy.

"The narrative is a true story that would be of interest to anyone curious about the history and practices of Jewish immigrants and their fate in the New World. This tale adds a touch of mystery as a very personal quest is undertaken to uncover a family secret concerning a long hidden death."

Dr. Fred Abrams is the author of *Doctors on the Edge: Will Your Doctor Break the Rules for You?* He is also the 2006 recipient of the Isaac Bell and John Hayes Award for Leadership in Medical Ethics and Professionalism from the American Medical Association.

"The Secrets They Kept is a heartrending true story of an observant Jewish family in the 1930s dealing with a tragic situation they kept buried for generations. As a result of Suzanne Handler's painstaking research to uncover her family's darkest secrets, readers are transported back to that era to discover the moral dilemmas they faced."

Richard Rheins, Senior Rabbi, Temple Sinai, Denver, Colorado

"Every murder has its secrets. Suzanne Handler has stumbled upon a decade's old family secret and reveals it to the world in her intriguing and compelling book. Her well-researched investigation into this family's tragic circumstance takes us on a journey through the social, religious and legal quagmires that existed in Wyoming, circa 1930. As a criminal defense attorney, I was especially interested in the procedures and process the accused traversed, as well as the conflict between the federal and local authorities as to how and where the matter would be tried, if at all. The author's inclusion of the federal judge's sound and eloquently reasoned decision, in its entirety, is a must read for anyone who faces the task of representing a seemingly indefensible case."

Philip Thornton, Attorney at Law, Tacoma, Washington

The Secrets They Kept

Robert Christiansen Jr.
TRUE CRIME

The Secrets They Kept

THE TRUE STORY OF A MERCY KILLING THAT SHOCKED A TOWN AND SHAMED A FAMILY

SUZANNE HANDLER

iLane PRESS

iLane Press

www.suzannehandler.com

Library of Congress Cataloging-in-Publication Data

Handler, Suzanne.
    The secrets they kept : the true story of a mercy killing that shocked a town and shamed a family / Suzanne Handler.
      p. cm.
    Includes bibliographical references.
    ISBN: 978-0-9885639-0-2 (pbk.)
    ISBN: 978-0-9885639-1-9 (e-book)
    1. Cheyenne (Wyo.)—Biography. 2. Killing of the mentally ill. 3. Trials (Murder). 4. Family secrets.   I. Title.
HV6515 .H36 2013
364.152—dc23

                                        2012956035

Cover and interior design: Eddie Iverson for Courant Creative

10 9 8 7 6 5 4 3 2 1

First Edition

In Memory of Sally
Rest in Peace

CONTENTS

ACKNOWLEDGEMENTS

Writing *The Secrets They Kept* was a challenging endeavor from start to finish. Many people paved the way with research, advice, and countless hours of editing, not to mention the occasional hand-holding as I cried and struggled through the painful process of revealing my family's hidden past.

First, I would like to thank Jerry Newman, my life partner of many years. Along with being my best friend and confidante, it was Jerry who drove me to Cheyenne on hot summer mornings and bitter, wind-swept afternoons so I might walk and re-walk the cemetery grounds where Sally lies. Jerry has listened to Sally's story so many times that I truly believe he knows each word and chapter by heart.

My sincere thanks also to the following individuals whose invaluable help made *The Secrets They Kept* a reality:

To Larry Brown, my amazing researcher at the Wyoming State Archives, without whose efforts this book simply could not have been written. Thank you for unlocking so many doors on my behalf.

To my cousin Kenneth, who had the wisdom to look for answers beyond mere words. Your search for the truth helped pave my way.

To my cousin Larry, who read Sally's story with such incredible empathy and compassion. Larry, I will always be grateful for your support and encouragement over these many years.

To Rabbi Richard Rheins: Your guidance in all matters of faith were immeasurable to the integrity of this book. Thank you for your time and wise counsel on this project.

A special thanks to my editor, Karen Albright Lin: Thank you for your ability to turn confusion into clarity, repetition into simplicity. I appreciate your dedication to my passion for bringing Sally's story to the written page.

And to all my friends and family: Your love and encouragement has kept me sane through the seemingly endless days and lonely nights of committing words to paper. A special thank you to Naomi Wisott, Alison Sandler, Cheryl Uhrmacher, and Sue Silberman.

Nearly last, but certainly not least, I would like to acknowledge my Aunt Virginia, the person who first revealed Sally's story to me. I am forever in your debt, for you made it all possible.

And finally to my mother, who, at the end of her life, blessed this book and all its contents. Thank you for giving me permission to share your secrets with the world.

PROLOGUE

"All families have their secrets, most people would never know them, but they know there are spaces, gaps where the answers should be, where someone should have sat, where someone used to be. A name that is never uttered, or uttered just once and never again. We all have our secrets."

– Cecelia Ahern, *The Book of Tomorrow*

The day began with such promise. Following my younger son's college graduation ceremony, my aunt and I were busy hanging paper streamers across my patio, creating a festive mood for a gathering that night in his honor. As often happened with this special person, I directed our conversation toward complaints about my mother and the difficult relationship she and I had shared for as long as I could remember. It was evident that I was angry and disappointed, this time by the fact that my parents had not come from California for their grandson's graduation. My aunt listened patiently as I began the familiar rant she had been privy to for years. Finally, in exasperation I am sure, she took my arm and ushered me back inside the house. As we sat together at my kitchen table that May afternoon, I learned an incredible piece of family history that has forever altered the course of my life.

"Suzanne, prepare yourself to be shocked by what I am going to tell you about your mother. Once you know the truth, I think you will understand her better."

She paused to see if anyone else, presumably my son, was within hearing range.

"I promised your uncle when I married into the family that I would never breathe a word of this and I have kept that promise until today."

What could be so dark, so ominous that my favorite aunt had been sworn to secrecy while still a bride? I couldn't imagine and didn't know what to expect. I waited, keenly aware of a thunderous pounding in my chest, every sense on high alert. She was about to tell me something of great importance about my mother, but what?

"Suzanne, your mother had a younger sister and her name was Sally."

"Sally?" I asked. "I never heard of a sister named Sally."

Slowly, this time in a voice barely above a whisper, my aunt continued: "Your Grandpa Sam killed her when she was about sixteen years old. He shot her somewhere outside Greeley, Colorado."

"He *killed* her?"

I shook my head in disbelief, unable to comprehend what I was hearing. My grandfather, the sweet old man who sang Yiddish tunes to my children when they were little? He shot and killed his own daughter? Impossible. Why would he have done such a thing? And who was Sally? It took awhile for the impact of my aunt's words to sink in, but when they did, the joy of my own child's graduation day evaporated like so much air escaping a punctured balloon.

I could hear my son and several of his friends laughing in the hallway. My aunt knew that I needed to know more about the incredible story she had just dropped in my lap, but just at that moment the young men entered the kitchen and that was the end of our conversation.

Later that evening, while the graduation party was well underway, my aunt pulled me aside and again, in a voice just above a whisper, reminded me I must never tell anyone that I knew there was once a sister named Sally and that my Grandpa Sam had killed her. The bizarre weekend passed in a blur. We never had another opportunity to discuss Sally or my grandfather again before my aunt returned to her California home. That night, and for many nights afterward, my thoughts returned to the image of my Grandpa Sam and his murdered daughter Sally—the girl with no face.

The secret shared with me on that day was short on explanation, but life changing to be sure. My grandfather, by then long deceased, had been the symbol of quiet strength and stability in our family and the one person I knew my mother admired above all others. She had adored Grandpa Sam, as had I. What, I kept asking myself, was I to do with this explosive information that threatened to destroy the fabric of my reality? What was my responsibility to myself and to the rest of my family, those whom I presumed were also unaware of this amazing story? Sally's life and unimaginable death was a secret I obviously wasn't supposed to know about, so I couldn't possibly question my mother. I reasoned that if she had wanted me to know about her sister, my mother would have certainly told me by now. Bound by my promise, I knew I would keep silent out of regard for my aunt. I told myself that one day, when the time was right, I would find out more about what happened on August 16, 1937, and why.

Life intervened and thoughts about Sally faded, but never entirely disappeared. Then, in 2003, as if it were ordained, I received a large package in the mail from one of my California cousins. Inside were copies of newspaper articles from the two Cheyenne daily papers about my mother's family that dated from August 16, 1937, through November of that same year. It appears my mother, for whatever reason, told this cousin about Sally. The two were extremely close, yet it still disturbs me that my mother shared her family's dark past with him, but never mentioned a word about it to me. Apparently my cousin's curiosity motivated him to investigate further. Upon receiving the requested articles, he then sent copies to several other relatives, including my mother and my one surviving uncle (husband of the aunt who first told me about Sally).

I quickly devoured each page, feeding my brain with dramatic tidbits of truth about my family's history. On a second, more careful read, I scoured every paragraph searching for key words and phrases that might unlock secrets about this mysterious relative who had died so long ago, yet continued to live in the shadow of my life. In how many ways, I wondered, had the tragedy of her life impacted my own?

The newspaper articles I held in my hands reported the heartbreaking events of August 16, 1937. I learned that Sally did not die outside Greeley, Colorado, as my aunt had said, but in Cheyenne, Wyoming, less than three miles from her home. One of the newspapers also reported that a murder-suicide pact between my grandfather and Sally had failed; that it had been my grandfather's intention to die alongside his child. The other daily paper stated my grandfather had been indicted for murder by a federal grand jury. I read on as if in a trance. It was then that I learned Sally had suffered from a "mental malady." What other ominous secrets were there to discover about my family's history? What had been left unsaid by the press, for surely there was much more to know about this strange tale? I read through the articles again and again, but nowhere among the pages was the most important question of all addressed to my satisfaction: What force in the universe would compel a father to shoot and kill his own child?

With daily thoughts of Sally racing through my head, I planned my annual trip to California. Knowing my mother had received the newspaper packet from my cousin, and that she also knew that I had read the very same articles, I arrived at her doorstep in the winter of 2003 armed with a myriad of questions: Who was Sally and what was she really like? What had happened to this girl in the days and weeks leading up to her death, and who in the family had made the decision to keep Sally's life and death a secret for all these years? And what of my grandfather's unimaginable crime? How could my mother have held her father in such high esteem knowing what he had done? I was ready for answers. Unfortunately, my mother was not prepared to give them, at least not to me.

Within the first hour of my arrival, my mother told me she had read the "material" sent by my cousin and then immediately burned it in her fireplace because "I never want to read or talk about this again!" I begged her to reconsider, but she flatly refused. Her pronouncement closed the window of opportunity for me on that particular visit, for I knew it was pointless to persist. My mother was secretive by nature and stubborn when she set her mind to something. Years of uncomfortable conversations on a variety of topics told me it was futile to persist. I would just have to wait.

The following year, 2004, I was even more resolved to find answers to the questions that played havoc with my mind by day and disturbed my sleep by night. I had reminded my mother numerous times during our weekly telephone conversations in the months leading up to my California trip that I intended to write her sister's story, with or without her cooperation. Her response was always vague; the hesitation in her voice spoke volumes. I understood that the road ahead would be difficult without her help. If necessary, I kept telling myself, I was prepared to make that uncomfortable journey alone.

Over the next three years, my mother and I had several discussions about Sally, and on one occasion she even produced a never-before-seen family picture that included her sister. Seeing Sally for the first time reduced me to tears. I looked into her small, dark face and was reminded again of the great tragedy of her untimely death. In each of these conversations, whether in person or on the telephone, it was apparent that when my mother spoke about Sally she did so reluctantly, always holding on to whatever painful memories and shameful secrets she had kept hidden for so long. Even as her health continued to decline and the end was growing near, I knew my mother was unwilling, or unable, to reveal all the details of what lead up to that fateful summer day. The time had come for me to honor her privacy and let the matter rest. In return, she gave me her permission to continue to search, on my own, for the truth as I saw fit.

Three days before my mother's death in 2007 we spoke of her sister Sally one last time. As I stood beside her hospital bed, her frail hand in mine, I made the promise that has become this book. I have told Sally's story and given voice, at last, to her long-forgotten life.

ONE

Murder in the Morning

"Proprietor of Store Takes Girl to City Limits
Where Shooting Occurs . . ."
–*Wyoming State Tribune*, August 16, 1937

He would murder his child. There was no other way.

Sam Levin was not a man of violence. He owned no weapon to carry out the promise he had made, the promise he intended to keep. A disembodied voice seemed to emanate from the walls of his modest home, or was it coming from inside his head? He wasn't quite sure anymore. It ordered him to "Do what you have to do! Kill her now!"

Trapped in a nightmare of indecision, held captive in a life or death tug-of-war not of his own making, Sam had wrestled with doubt for days and nights without end. He knew the unspeakable act he was about to commit was wrong, but what other choice did he have? Plagued by agonizing thoughts, exhausted from plaintive prayer, Sam heard the clock in the narrow hallway tick away the final hours before his beloved Sally would be taken from him, perhaps never to return. At last he decided: father and daughter would die together, partners in a plan devised to end the torment of sleepless nights that yawned and stretched before them, taunting them both with yet another tomorrow. A tomorrow neither could endure.

The first innocent rays of sunlight streaked across the midsummer sky, witness-in-waiting to a crime that would shock a town and bring shame upon a family for decades. The smell of death was everywhere. Sam could not escape it.

Sighing deeply for what seemed like the hundredth time that morning, Sam repeatedly checked his ancient pocket-watch and waited for 10 a.m., the hour he knew the pawnshops in town would open and begin their daily business of receiving the once coveted treasures of the rich and the ragtag artifacts of the debt-ridden poor. At 9:45 a.m., unable to wait another minute, Sam rushed out the door and headed for his truck, eager to complete the first step in his plan— a deadly blueprint to destroy that which he loved most.

A reverie of happier days flooded his ravaged mind: sweet moments when father and daughter, hand-in-hand, had walked the short blocks to the neighborhood grocery store for freshly-baked bread; late summer afternoons fishing together in the nearby lake with Sally and her older sister; Sally's good-by kiss as she headed off to school each morning with sugary crumbs from her glazed doughnut still clinging to her lips. Those days, Sam knew, were gone forever. All that remained was the bitter taste of unrelenting sadness, mingled with tears he was powerless to control.

At the pawnshop, with little knowledge of guns, Sam made what looked to be a reasonable choice: an old-style Harrington and Richardson .32 caliber revolver. Although the $3.00 price seemed excessive, there was no time on that particular morning to quibble. He quickly paid the bill and hurried from the shop. The merchant knew Sam; many of the shopkeepers in downtown Cheyenne knew Sam. He was one of them, a store owner struggling to coax a meager living from the clenched jaws of their financially strapped town, a town limping its way through the waning years of the Great Depression. Did the pawnbroker suspect something was amiss, that a terrible crime was about to be committed?

The determined father climbed into his truck and drove the few short miles back home, darting around corners to avoid recognition by townspeople he knew. Only weeks before, he had been proud to display his name and second-hand furniture business for all to see: the modicum of success he had achieved in this, his adopted homeland. That was then. Today was different. He could not allow himself to consider the shame, the disgrace his name would come to symbolize once this day was done. Sam forced himself to concentrate on the road before him, willed himself to abandon the dark thoughts that pushed and shoved their way into his head. But it was no use. He could not escape the memory of the moment when denial of Sally's "malady" had morphed into grim reality. That was the day the words "incurable" and "insane asylum" had torn his once ordinary life to shreds.

Sam suspected that Sally, his youngest daughter and source of his relentless pain and unabated sorrow, heard his heavy footsteps as they scraped the pavement leading from the driveway to their front door. Did she know the end was near? Sam entered the house to find his daughter poised on the edge of their tattered sofa. There the girl sat, nervously wringing her hands and mumbling incoherent phrases under her breath, her face a twisted mask that Sam could not decipher. As if this anguished father needed further reminder of the obligation that loomed before him, the voice in his head—his uninvited companion these many days and sleepless nights—urged him once again to "Go ahead! Kill her now!"

Momentarily unsure of his decision, Sam hesitated. He looked down at Sally, the child for whom his heart now ached, and knew he must grant her wish to die. But how, he wondered, could he possibly explain the enormity of what he was about to do, not just to family members they would soon leave behind, but also to the world beyond his front door? Sam thought about the citizens of the town who had embraced him so fondly. He wanted them to understand the wellspring of his actions. At that moment, the beleaguered father decided to write a note of explanation, not in English, for on this day such words failed him, but rather in Yiddish, the language of his birth.

Sam gently helped Sally to a standing position, her body stiff and unyielding beneath his strong fingers, and guided her toward the kitchen table. Choking back tears, he took paper and pencil in hand and scribbled the lines that sealed their fate: a death-pact promise that they would die together. After signing both their names, Sam stuffed the note in his pants pocket next to the small pocketknife he always carried. Then, in a gruff voice designed to disguise his fear and overwhelming sorrow, he told Sally that it was time to go. Together, they walked through their front door for the last time. Sam silently prayed to the God of his people he would not lose his courage when the time came. Most of all, he prayed to be forgiven for what he was about to do.

Sometime before 11 a.m. that morning, father and daughter drove to a remote location west of Cheyenne's city limits, halfway between Highway 36 and Happy Jack Road. What happened during that short drive? Did either express regret? Did tearful lamentations prevail or did stony silence envelope parent and child in a shroud of their eventual doom? Upon reaching what Sam perceived to be the perfect spot, totally isolated from view and void of any curious onlookers, the two climbed down from the truck and stood a few feet in front of the vehicle. It was there, at close range, that Sam raised his trembling hand and shot Sally once in the left temple and once in the right breast. The sound of gunshots exploded in Sam's ears and then there was silence. The girl immediately collapsed and fell to the ground, blood gushing from her wounds. Had there been hesitation in those last few seconds before this tormented father glanced into the eyes of his daughter one last time? Or, did both lost souls remain resolute until the end? What words, if any, were spoken just seconds before there would be no turning back?

While Sally lay crumpled on the ground before him, Sam took aim at his own head and fired twice. The first bullet grazed his forehead and lodged in the windshield of his truck. The second bullet entered his left cheek near the bone and forced him to his knees. With each shot, a loud boom again punctured the air, followed immediately by a momentary pause. Then nothing stirred at all. Still conscious, and perspiring profusely, Sam pleaded with God to let him die. As a final measure, Sam fumbled for his pocketknife and, with blood running down his face and onto his shirt, stabbed his chest multiple times. With each thrust, he told himself that living without Sally was something he could not, he would not do.

As the critically injured girl lay gasping for each breath, Sam knew, without question, that his child would soon die. But why, he asked himself, did he still live? Had God failed to hear his prayers on this day? Or, as punishment for his crime, had He simply chosen not to answer them?

Less than 200 yards from the spot where copious amounts of blood had been shed, two men were whiling away the morning digging for fish worms. Alerted by the sound of gunshots nearby, the men ran to where both father and daughter lay on the ground, approximately five feet from Sam's delivery truck. According to an account the next morning in *The Wyoming Eagle* (August 17, 1937), one of the men said, "We walked up to where Levin was lying and I asked him what was going on. He was able to talk and he (Sam) said, 'there's been a murder and suicide, call the police, call somebody. I killed her and tried to kill myself, but I shot too high, then I tried to stab myself.'"

A flurry of activity followed. One of the men drove the short distance into town and informed the authorities that a crime had been committed and that an ambulance was needed immediately. By the time the deputy sheriff and the acting police chief arrived, it was evident that Sally was close to death. As if to explain the gruesome sight before them, Sam pulled the murder-suicide note written earlier that morning from his pocket and handed it to the deputy. Nobody in the stunned group could decipher the words. The note that was later translated from Yiddish to English by a friend of the family read as follows:

My dear friends

I am going to do this because I do not want to go to Evanston (the Wyoming State Hospital). I have the same sickness as my daughter Sally. It is only a matter of a few days that it will be necessary to watch me. So all be well my wife, my daughter and my sons.

I ask my sons to take care of Mother. Goodbye.

I ask . . . he should help my family and I give my sons an advice that they should move to another city when they have everything straightened out. From Me.

Sam and Sally

Two weeks shy of her seventeenth birthday, Sally Levin's life ended. The headline in the *Wyoming State Tribune* (August 16, 1937) that evening screamed the horrible news:

"CHEYENNE FATHER KILLS DAUGHTER, 17, AND THEN SHOOTS AND STABS HIMSELF"

So there it was for all to see and know: the climactic end to a murder that defied explanation—at least on first blush. A quiet man, a gentle man, a man who cherished his family above all else had, in a matter of minutes, torn it asunder. The agony he must have suffered before and after condemning them both to death is unimaginable. Sally died at the hospital within the hour. Sam survived his injuries and lived to celebrate his eighty-eighth birthday.

Sam Levin was my grandfather and his youngest daughter, Sally, was my aunt. Since learning about Sally's life and her unfathomable death, I have asked myself many times: Who was this person I had loved so much throughout my childhood? How could he have taken away that which was so dear to him? According to court records and newspaper accounts, it was an irrefutable fact that my grandfather's love for Sally was so profound, and his own emotional state so fragile, that he felt compelled to end her life in accordance with her expressed wish to die. It is also true that my grandfather carried the details of Sally's downward spiral into the dark pit of her mental illness, and what I can only imagine as the terrifying moments before her death, to his grave.

UNITED STATES

STATE OF WYOMING
CERTIFICATE OF DEATH

BUREAU VITAL STATISTICS
CAPITOL BUILDING
CHEYENNE, WYOMING

1. PLACE OF DEATH
County *Laramie*

Township *Cheyenne* Registration Dist. No. *1*
No. *Memorial Hosp* Street

City *Cheyenne*
(If death occurred in hospital or institution, give its name instead of street and number)

Do Not Write in This Space
File No. 1937 1625
Registered No.

Length of residence in city or town where death occurred *life* yrs. mos. days How long in U. S. if of foreign birth? yrs. mos. days

2. FULL NAME *Sally Lewin*

(a) Residence: No. *1001 E 20* St., Ward
(Usual place of abode) (If non-resident, give city or town and State)

PERSONAL AND STATISTICAL PARTICULARS

MEDICAL CERTIFICATE OF DEATH

3. SEX *Fr.* 4. COLOR or RACE *W* 5. Single, Married, Widowed, or Divorced (write the word) *single*

5a. If married, widowed, or divorced
HUSBAND of
(or) WIFE of *Sept 6*

6. DATE OF BIRTH (month, day, and year)

7. AGE Years *16* Months Days If LESS than 1 day ...hrs. or ...min.

8. Trade, profession, or particular kind of work done, as spinner, sawyer, bookkeeper, etc. *at school*

9. Industry or business in which work was done, as silk mill, saw mill, bank, etc.

10. Date deceased last worked at this occupation (month and year)

11. Total time (years) spent in this occupation

12. BIRTHPLACE (city or town) *Cheyenne Wyo*
(State or country)

13. NAME *Sam Lewin*

14. BIRTHPLACE (city or town) *Russia*
(State or country)

15. MAIDEN NAME

16. BIRTHPLACE (city or town) *Russia*
(State or country)

17. INFORMANT *Archie Lewin*
(Address) *Cheyenne Wyo*

18. BURIAL, CREMATION, OR REMOVAL *Jewish Cem* Place *Aug 17 37*

19. UNDERTAKER *Paul Albotan*
(Address) *Cheyenne*

20. FILED *Aug 17 1937* M.R.L. *Reg Magistrat*

21. DATE OF DEATH (month, day and year) *Aug 16 37*

22. I HEREBY CERTIFY, That I attended deceased from 19 to 19

I last saw h.... alive on 19, death is said to have occurred on the date stated above, at *11:45 AM*.

The principal cause of death and related causes of importance were as follows: *Gunshot wound in head and chest*

DATE OF ONSET

Other contributory causes of importance:

Name of operation *Physical find'g*
What test confirmed diagnosis? Was there an autopsy? *No*
22. If death was due to external causes (violence) fill in also the following:
Accident, suicide, or homicide? *homicide* Date of injury *Aug 16 37*
Where did injury occur? *1 mi e of Cheyenne*
(Specify city or town, county, and State)
Specify whether injury occurred in industry, in home, or in public place. *on highway*
Manner of injury *homicide*
Nature of injury
Was disease or injury in any way related to occupation of deceased? If so, specify

(Signed) *Paul Albotan* Coroner M. D.
(Address) *Cheyenne Wyo.*

Sally's Death Certificate
—Wyoming State Archives

Eagle Photo and Engraving

The Levin Tragedy

was discovered by the two men shown in the upper picture kneeling at the place where Sam Levin shot his daughter and then attempted to kill himself. They are Frank Baird (left) and Francis Stamy. In the lower picture Detective Harvey Jackson points to a bullet hole in the windshield of the car in which the man and his daughter drove to the outskirts of the city. The hole was made by the bullet that creased Levin's scalp. Another hole in the rear window was made by a bullet that he fired at himself and missed.

–The Wyoming Eagle, August 18, 1937

–The Wyoming Eagle, August 18, 1937

TWO

Collateral Damage

"Truth of Levin Tragedy Kept From Grief-Stricken Mother"
–*The Wyoming Eagle*, August 19, 1937

Rather than waste precious minutes waiting for the ambulance to arrive, father and daughter were placed in Sam's delivery truck for the short trip to Cheyenne's Memorial Hospital. Although bloodied and weak from his wounds, Sam managed to walk to his vehicle unaided. Carefully, almost reverently, the unconscious Sally, her labored breathing deteriorating by the second, was positioned in the back of the truck. The entire group then took off at record speed for town where they soon met up with the ambulance. As Sally's limp body was transferred from her father's truck to the waiting emergency vehicle, there appeared little chance the girl would survive. Sam remained in his truck, driven by one of the men who had discovered the crime scene. Upon reaching the hospital, Sam lumbered slowly, yet on his own volition, to a waiting stretcher. He had resigned himself to the knowledge that, in spite of their death pact to end their lives together, he would live to bear witness to his beloved daughter's death and his role as her murderer.

At the hospital, Sam was immediately placed under police guard. Lying on a cot next to his barely breathing child, the physically and emotionally exhausted father fell into a deep sleep. When he awoke he was told that Sally had died and that her body had already been taken to the morgue. The time was 11:55 a.m.—less than one hour from the moment she was shot. One of Sam's doctors later reported, "He (Sam) believes his daughter's death (to be) a divine act." (*The Wyoming Eagle*, August 17, 1937)

It was not long before Sam descended into a deep state of melancholia, relieved that he had fulfilled his daughter's wish, but also despondent that his plan, at least in part, had failed. He was alive, and that was not how he had imagined the situation would end. The doctors, aware of his depression and his fervent wish to die, placed Sam under a suicide watch, fearful he might make a second attempt to end his life.

Within hours of Sally's passing, a coroner's jury was convened. According to a newspaper account that evening in the *Wyoming State Tribune* (August 16, 1937), the verdict, by unanimous decision, read as follows:

"We the jury find that Sally Levin died at 11:55 a.m., August 16, as a result of gunshot wounds to her head and chest inflicted by one Sam Levin. We are convinced by the testimony of Dr. W. K. Mylar and Dr. W. A. Bunton (two local physicians) that said Sam Levin was insane when he committed the act and therefore cannot be held responsible for it."

Soon after the coroner's verdict was issued, the county prosecutor announced a sanity hearing would be held in several days. If my grandfather were found insane at the time of that hearing, he would have been automatically sent to Evanston—the state insane asylum in Wyoming where Sally would have been committed had she lived. If not found insane, my grandfather would stand trial for murder, which is exactly what happened.

News of Sally Levin's death, and my grandfather's role as her murderer, spread quickly through the small town and tongues were wagging in anticipation of the evening edition of the newspaper. Meanwhile, in an apparent attempt to protect my grandmother from the truth, she was told her daughter and husband had been in a serious automobile accident. To further soften the blow, the distraught woman was informed that Sally had died as a result of her injuries and that Sam was in serious condition. No one mentioned anything about murder, a suicide attempt, or a signed death pact.

There were reports that my grandmother was taken to the hospital soon after Sally and Sam were admitted, but she arrived too late to say good-by to her child. *The Wyoming Eagle* stated in its headline on the morning of August 19th that the "Truth of Levin Tragedy Kept from Grief-Stricken Mother" and when anyone calls to offer condolences they are told by family members, "She does not know."

My most vivid memory of my grandmother is of her sitting in a straight-back chair looking out the window for hours on end. Try as I might, I have absolutely no recollection of ever having a conversation with her beyond a simple "hello." Is it possible that when she finally learned the truth about the great tragedy that had befallen her family, perhaps sometime after Sally's funeral and the lengthy mourning period that followed, my grandmother simply slipped away from reality as a way of dealing with her great loss?

As for my mother, 1,000 miles away in Los Angeles, her grief and guilt would come later and last a lifetime. Sometime past noon, after Sally's body already lay in the morgue, her death certificate signed and sealed, my mother received a Western Union Telegram urging her to "Come home immediately. Sally dangerously ill." The individual who sent this message has never been identified.

Dr. Mylar, who along with Dr. Bunton, would play a prominent role in determining the outcome of my grandfather's case, stated to the evening newspaper (*Wyoming State Tribune*, August 16, 1937) that "He (Sam) hopes he will die (soon) and that his love for the girl prompted him to take her life." Dr. Mylar continued: "He (Sam) couldn't stand to live without her. Levin has been unable to sleep the last three days. It is typical that an act of violence results from such a mental state." Dr. Bunton, in speaking to the same reporter, added that Sam "had disclosed at the hospital after the shooting that he was a victim of the same 'mental malady' as his daughter."

Three months after Sally's death, an officer of the court would tell the judge that when he interviewed my grandfather days before his sentencing, Sam had told him, " . . . when he found himself in the hospital on a cot beside the cot on which Sally lay and heard the doctor announce that she was dead, he experienced a sense of relief that he did not know how to describe, and which he was sure if he did, no one would understand. He had carried out her desires and his only disappointment was that he had failed in his attempt to go with her."

On the morning of August 17th, the day after the murder, the headline in *The Wyoming Eagle* read as follows:

"DEATH PACT BARED IN LEVIN 'MERCY' SLAYING"

The sensational and partially incorrect subtext read: "Father, Near Death, Says Insanity Drove Both to Agreement." In truth, Sam remained in serious, but not critical condition. The two stab wounds to his chest were superficial, deflected by a rib. Of the two gunshots fired to his head, one merely grazed his scalp and lodged in the windshield of his delivery truck. The other required surgery, as the bullet was embedded in my grandfather's cheek. This procedure took place on the afternoon of August 17th and left a small scar that I vaguely recall seeing as a child.

It was on this day after the crime that the morning newspaper first used the terms "mercy slaying" and "insanity" in conjunction with my grandfather's crime, but it would not be the last. Sally's mental condition was revealed in slightly more detail by Dr. Bunton, who is quoted in the *The Wyoming Eagle* (August 17, 1937) as saying, "I examined her (Sally) a week ago and she was suffering from dementia praecox (schizophrenia). In this condition persons are suspicious of others and often feel that others are planning to do them bodily harm. Quite often they are suspicious of members of their own families. Oftentimes such sufferers think they are connected to the deity and feel they must carry out orders they presume are of the deity."

By the close of this second day, Sam's morbid thoughts of his own demise had been replaced by a faint glimmer of remorse for what he had done. It is also likely my grandfather realized from that point forward he would forever be known as Cheyenne's disgraced "mercy slayer."

As details of the story began to emerge, it appears that my grandfather, confused and overwhelmed by the nature of Sally's illness, and fearful that her strange behaviors might endanger her or other family members, first sought advice from county prosecutor Richard Caldwell. Mr. Caldwell suggested Sam take Sally to Dr. Bunton, one of the town's most highly respected physicians. This appointment took place 7–10 days before her death. Following his own examination and diagnosis of dementia praecox, Dr. Bunton then referred Sam and Sally to a psychiatrist in Denver, Colorado who made a similar diagnosis. While in Denver, according to court records, Sally experienced an "episode" and, as a result, spent a week in a private mental hospital in that city. Both doctors eventually conferred and agreed Sally was incurable and "potentially dangerous," according to *The Wyoming Eagle* (August 17, 1937). The next step was to sign the papers necessary to commit Sally to the Wyoming State Hospital in Evanston.

In the time between their return from Denver and the day of her death, Sally must have been lucid enough to comprehend that her commitment to Evanston was inevitable and exactly what that meant. It is likely that it was during this period, or perhaps even on the long drive back from Denver to Cheyenne, that Sally begged her father to end her life rather than send her to Evanston, a town over 300 miles from their Cheyenne home. It is well within the range of possibility that Sally's death plea was motivated by feelings of disgrace about her illness, her deeply depressed state, and terrifying thoughts of separation from her family. According to *The Wyoming Eagle* (August 17, 1937), "The girl had brooded over her illness and appeared unusually despondent to her friends." The newspaper, however, did not mention any specific behaviors or incidents that would have resulted in a diagnosis of dementia praecox, a disease that few people in Cheyenne had even heard of, much less understood.

Sally had a relative who had spent much of her life in an institution for the mentally challenged and she (Sally) was aware of the stigma attached to this condition. This individual's handicap, according to my mother, was well known in the small Jewish community (approximately 150 families in 1935) and had been discussed often within the walls of the Levin family home. Such knowledge may have added to Sally's distress and my grandfather's determination to honor his daughter's wish to die. There was such a tremendous sense of shame and fear, especially in those years, when a family member was diagnosed with a mental illness or handicap. The workings of a diseased mind were a mystery to most, and a bewildering situation many families would have hidden from view. It is probable that my mother's family was no exception.

My grandfather was an orthodox Jew. As he lay recovering in his hospital bed, he knew funeral plans were underway to bury his daughter on that very day as it was, and still is, customary in the Jewish faith to inter their deceased quickly. In Jewish funeral rites, embalming is forbidden, thus a speedy burial is mandatory. Although he was physically a little stronger on this second day, Sam's wish to participate in Sally's funeral service was never an option. The police guard and the hospital aide stationed near his bedside confirmed that fact.

As regrets for Sally's death continued to escalate in his mind, my grandfather must have struggled mightily with the knowledge that he would not be at his daughter's grave site to recite the traditional Mourner's Kaddish. This 2,000 year-old prayer, composed of Aramaic and Hebrew meditations, is recited at all Jewish burials both to honor the dead and to reaffirm the sanctity of life. It reads as follows:

Glorified and sanctified be God's great name throughout the world which He has created according to His will. May He establish His kingdom in your lifetime and during your days, and within the life of the entire House of Israel, speedily and soon; and say, Amen. May His great name be blessed forever and to all eternity. Blessed and praised, glorified and exalted, extolled and honored, adored and lauded be the name of the Holy One, blessed be He, beyond all the blessings and hymns, praises and consolations that are ever spoken in the world; and say, Amen. May there be abundant peace from heaven, and life, for us and for all Israel; and say, Amen. He who creates peace in His celestial heights, may He create peace for us and for all Israel; and say, Amen.

Immediately following Sally's funeral, it was assumed that any judicial proceedings would be held in Laramie County Court, which includes the city of Cheyenne. All that changed when it was discovered the murder had actually taken place 75 feet within the boundary of Fort Warren, a federal military reservation on the outskirts of

Cheyenne. This juicy piece of front-page news placed the case under the jurisdiction of the federal court system, and added considerable fodder for gossip among the townspeople. While still hospitalized and under police guard, my grandfather was served a federal warrant and charged with manslaughter for "unlawfully, knowingly and fully without malice," taking the life of his child. Several prominent Jewish businessmen posted the bail required for my grandfather's release. Ten days after Sally's death, my grandfather was allowed to return home. He would never spend a day in jail for the crime he had committed.

A House of Tragedy is the building pictured here. This is the house at 1001 E. 20th owned by Sam Levin, Cheyenne merchant who fatally wounded his daughter and then attempted to commit suicide after making a mercy death pact with the girl.

–The Wyoming Eagle, August 18, 1937

THREE

"Dust to Dust"

"Dust thou art, and unto dust thou shalt return."
–Genesis 3:19

The infamous Wyoming wind howled through the man-made canyons of the deserted cemetery on that late winter afternoon as I trudged up and down row after row of graves, straining to read the words inscribed on each snow-covered plaque. At last I stood before a small, unadorned headstone bearing the name of my long-forgotten relative: Sally Levin. I had found what I was looking for, confirmation of a painfully brief life and an incredibly horrific death. A rush of tears slid down my frozen cheeks and pooled in the collar of my jacket. Shivering from the biting cold that permeated my winter coat as if it were tissue paper, I bowed my head in silent tribute to the 16-year-old girl who lay in eternal repose, and for the disturbing conditions that led to her death. What secrets of her life and my family were buried beneath this frozen, unforgiving patch of earth, this hallowed place of sorrow and regret?

The tears kept coming, and though I furiously wiped at them with my gloved hands, I was helpless to stop their flow. It was time to leave the cemetery; I had accomplished my mission. Yet for some reason, I couldn't pull myself away. I leaned in closer to read the simple inscription on Sally's headstone one last time. To my great amazement, I realized that her name, the most basic validation of Sally's days on earth, was misspelled as "Salie." Who had made this error and why had the mistake gone unnoticed all these many years?

Sally rests alone in her solitary world of the dead, for within a few short months following her death my family turned its back on all they once knew and loved, including Sally, and moved to Southern California. Although the cemetery was less than a mile from their home, my mother insisted no family members ever visited Sally's grave in the days, weeks, or even years, following her burial. Now, more than seven decades later, I am left to ponder the passing of one for whom life held so little promise and the answers to questions that have slipped away with the passage of time and memory.

Did townspeople, both Jews and Gentiles, weep for the girl who died by her father's hand? How many people gathered on that hot August afternoon to witness the descent of her young body into the gaping earth below? Nobody knows. What I do know is that, for obvious reasons, my grandfather was not there. Nor was my mother. She was visiting her older sister in California and would arrive the next day, less than twenty-four hours after Sally's body had already been committed to her grave.

Before a Jewish funeral can take place, certain rituals must be performed, each designed to properly prepare the deceased for his or her final journey. According to Jewish law and tradition, members of the Chevra Kadisha (Holy Society or Sacred Burial Society) from my grandfather's synagogue would have preformed these time-honored tasks. With great respect and dignity, Sally's body would have been carefully washed (*tahara*), dressed in a simple white shroud (known as *takhrikhin*), and placed in an unadorned, wooden casket. Once the casket was closed, Sally's body would never again be viewed.

Jewish funerals are traditionally held between twenty-four and forty-eight hours after death. In Sally's case, the funeral took place thirty hours after her passing. In the hours between the closing of her casket and the lowering of her body into the ground, Sally would never have been left alone. This practice of guarding the body *(shemira)* until burial is believed to bring honor to the deceased and is generally performed by a family member or someone from the funeral home if a relative is not available.

Following a brief service at The Worland Chapel on August 16, 1937, Sally Levin was buried in the Jewish cemetery in Cheyenne, Wyoming. The majority of mourners on that sad day would have been Sally's immediate and extended family. The recent notoriety and shame (*shanda*) associated with the family's name may have kept some would-be mourners from attending the funeral service or the graveside burial that followed. Stunned disbelief was most likely rampant among the Jewish population soon after the local newspapers identified Sam Levin as Sally's "mercy slayer." There were a number of friends and neighbors who, from the moment they learned what happened, never spoke to my grandfather again. In the three months that passed between Sally's funeral and my grandfather's trial, some of these individuals would cross the street to avoid eye contact with him and, it has been reported, instructed their children to do the same.

After the burial, family members would have made their way to the house, a short drive from the cemetery. One seven-day candle would have been lit in anticipation of the family's arrival and it would have remained lit for the entire seven-day mourning period known as *shiva* (seven, as in seven days). In most instances, all first-degree relatives—the father (although not in this case), mother, sisters and brothers—would have been considered official mourners, and would have been at the home to offer support to each other and to receive any visitors who had come to pay their respects. These official mourners would have had an article of their clothing torn (*keriah*) while still at the burial site, probably before the service began. This tearing ritual serves to remind the family, and all visitors to the home, that the death of their loved one has torn away part of their heart.

The atmosphere in any orthodox house of *shiva*, at least in those days, would have been dark and gloomy. All the mirrors in the home would have been covered, voices hushed. Twice each day during the *shiva* period, prayers would have been recited by a *minyan* (minimum) of ten Jewish males over the age of thirteen. Those considered official mourners would have sat on low stools, or perhaps the floor, as a public demonstration of their bereavement.

No one knows who orchestrated Sally's *shiva*. Because my grandfather was not there, and the family's rabbi was on vacation, it is probable that my grandmother's brother was in charge. As immigrants, the tone and details of the funeral and the *shiva* would have most likely been a reflection of Jewish funeral customs from their native Russia.

Upon receiving the telegram that read: "Come home immediately. Sally dangerously ill," my mother quickly arranged for her return to Cheyenne. Following my mother's death, I had an opportunity to speak with the childhood friend who met my mother at the train station on the day of her arrival. She said, "I picked your mother up and on the way to her house I told her that Sally was already dead and buried." My mother, according to this friend, was stoic at the news. Is it possible that my mother already knew, or suspected, that Sally's death was imminent before she left town?

Whether or not my mother's older sister returned to Cheyenne at the same time as my mother is a matter of conjecture. One newspaper account has them both arriving by train, another has them flying home. The truth is that this oldest sister was estranged from my grandparents at the time of Sally's death and it is highly unlikely that she would have been welcomed in the Levin home. I was only able to verify my mother's return to Cheyenne and that her best friend drove her home. It is impossible to imagine my mother's emotional state as she walked through the door and into the arms of her grieving family.

The purpose of "sitting" *shiva* is to provide a structured environment for the family to reflect, remember, and honor their loved one in the privacy of their own home. In the long days that followed the funeral, day-to-day life in the Levin household would have been suspended. As gossip and speculation continued to consume the attention of the local townspeople, reporters gathered outside the house waiting to ply new arrivals with questions. Tucked away in their secluded world, family members must have pondered my grandfather's fate, and to some extent, their own. It is unlikely that my mother, or any of her siblings for that matter, read the local papers or listened to the radio during this time. Any news beyond their door would have been delivered secondhand from visitors to the house. As the end of the mourning period approached, each family member surely contemplated his or her return to the real world with a mixture of both dread and relief. For the youngest child, a fifteen-year old boy about to enter high school in a matter of weeks, it must have been an especially difficult scenario to consider. This youngest sibling was the brother who, more than seventy years after her death, refused to ever discuss Sally's life with me.

It is not uncommon for immigrant communities to keep to themselves and to endure their collective sorrow and shame in private. Jews, who for over two millennia have been tortured, ghettoized, murdered, humiliated, and expelled from many lands for their religious beliefs and customs, have learned that avoiding negative attention is important to their survival. Because this particular case was made so public in the press, and because its very nature was so controversial, the Levin tragedy was on everyone's lips.

When news of Sally's death reached the general population of Cheyenne, many Jews worried that the reputation of their people would be slandered. It mattered little that my grandfather was past president of the Jewish Council of Cheyenne and had, until the day of Sally's death, been a merchant in good standing. Sam Levin had committed an unforgivable act and there was concern that the relationship between Jews and Gentiles in the small town could be in jeopardy. Recalling lines in my grandfather's suicide note, it is evident that he too understood that after August 16th nothing would ever be the same when he wrote: " . . . *I give my sons an advice that they should move to another city when they have everything straightened out.*"

My grandfather's advice to leave Cheyenne "when they (his surviving family) have everything straightened out" left little doubt as to his intention. It did not, however, take into account the question of who would order and dedicate either Sally's grave marker or his own. The placement of a headstone or grave marker at a grave site has been a Jewish custom for thousands of years. Is it possible my grandfather never considered this important tradition when he made his decision to end both their lives?

Jewish law requires that a grave marker be prepared so that the deceased will not be forgotten and the grave will not be desecrated. It is customary for the marker to be put in place and for an unveiling ceremony to be held at the end of (or near) the twelve-month mourning period. The idea underlying this custom is that the dead will not be forgotten when he (or she) is being mourned every day. The unveiling ceremony consists of the recitation of Psalms, a very brief eulogy and removing the cloth covering the headstone. It is also customary, before leaving the grave site, to place a small stone on the marker to indicate that someone has visited the grave. (*The Shiva House, Inc.*)

Since my grandfather and his family had left Cheyenne by the end of December 1937, it is unknown who ordered and paid for Sally's grave marker. Sally's headstone is simple, in keeping with the

Jewish tradition that commemorating the dead should be respectful and dignified. The few words that tell of her time on earth reveal nothing of her unfortunate life. Although many Jewish headstones read, in Hebrew, "May his (her) soul be bound in the biding of life" or "Here is buried," Sally's does not. It says only:

Salie Levin

Daughter

1920–1937

Have curious cemetery visitors passed by this burial site and stopped to wonder what happened to the young girl who rests here? Remembering my mother's words that "No one ever visited Sally's grave in the weeks, months, or years after Sally's death," I remain curious about something that happened a very long time ago. I was married with two young children in 1969 when my recently remarried grandfather (my grandmother died in 1962) paid a short visit to Denver. Sitting at my kitchen table watching our toddlers at play, my grandfather asked my husband to take him up to Cheyenne the next day for a visit. Following their trip, I learned that after a quick drive through town, the two men headed for the Jewish cemetery. My husband said he waited about 15 minutes outside the cemetery gates, as requested, and that when my grandfather returned to the car he never told my husband whose grave he was visiting or why. I would like to believe that in a somber moment of quiet reflection, my grandfather hung his head and begged Sally's forgiveness, and in doing so he was able to grant himself a brief moment of peace.

Sally's Grave Marker

CITY PERMIT № 7311

CITY OF CHEYENNE, WYOMING
BURIAL PERMIT

Cheyenne, Wyo., August 18, 1937

The City of Cheyenne hereby grants permission to........Paul H. Worland

to inter, in Lot.......................................Jewish........................Cemetery, the body of

....Sally Levin..Age...16.......Sex...Female

Color...White.........Cause of death...Gunshot wound in head and chest

Date of Death....August 16, 1937........Place of Death....Cheyenne, Wyoming

Attendant Physician..Paul H. Worland, Coroner....Undertaker....Paul H. Worland

Received $..None............payment in full for
opening and closing grave in City Cemetery.

Opening and closing by man employed by Jewish
people as caretaker in their Cemetery.

_____
Assistant City Treasurer

_____ City Clerk

Sally's Burial Permit
—Dorothy Feldman, Mt. Sinai Congregation

FOUR

The Girl They Called "Blackie"

"He Couldn't Stand to Live Without Her"
–*Wyoming State Tribune*, August 16, 1937

In 1937, millionaire Howard Hughes flew 7 hours and 28 minutes to set a transcontinental record, the Golden Gate Bridge opened to pedestrian and automobile traffic, and Adolph Hitler's diabolical plan to dominate Europe was well on its way to becoming reality. Meanwhile, in small-town Cheyenne, Wyoming, headlines about the bizarre death of a young woman riveted a community for months.

Who was Sally Levin? Was she like many teenage girls of her era, obsessed with jukeboxes, swing music, bobby sox, long skirts, and malted milks? Did she harbor a secret crush on a boy from her neighborhood, synagogue, or school? Did she dream of one day being a famous somebody, living far from her provincial home? Unfortunately, little is known about this girl. Shy and withdrawn, information about Sally has been obscured by the secrecy that surrounds her early death. I have but one small photo, one clue that speaks to me daily. It is this sad, dilapidated family picture that calls me to tell her story and by doing so, better understand my own.

Sally Levin (her Hebrew name was Sarah) was born in Cheyenne, Wyoming in 1920, the fourth of five siblings and my mother's youngest sister. My immigrant grandparents (Russian Jews) raised their children in a religiously observant home where the Sabbath was faithfully observed, dietary rules known as *Kashrut* (Kosher) were strictly followed, and religious services at the oldest synagogue in the state were regularly attended. The children understood the social norms of their tightly bound community and what was expected of them. Straying from the fold was rare.

Were there early signs that the events of August 16, 1937, were bubbling in an emotion-laden cauldron just beneath the surface in the Levin household? Mental illness was an off-limits topic of conversation because it was strange and frightening and, of course, because it was misunderstood. If there were signs, I suspect they were carefully hidden behind closed doors.

Sally was an average student, quiet and practically friendless at school. My mother told me that her sister had no serious learning problems, but that school was not especially easy or pleasant for her. I made several attempts to obtain Sally's school records, however, the city of Cheyenne does not keep such files unless a student graduates. As Sally died just weeks before she was to begin her junior year in high school, I was unable to glean anything about her academic life. Given my mother's description, it's possible that Sally spent the majority of her time at school trying her best not to be noticed. Her shyness would have kept her tethered to the few friends she had known since early childhood, the ones who didn't judge or ridicule her for being different. It would appear Sally was close to her siblings, even though they ranged in age from fifteen to twenty-six.

At the time of Sally's death, six members of the Levin family lived in a small, two-bedroom house, not far from a city park. My grandparents held claim on one bedroom. In the other, Sally's two brothers, ages fifteen and twenty-four slept in one bed and my mother and Sally, ages twenty-two and sixteen, slept in the other. Before the upheaval of her elopement to a Gentile and their move to California, the eldest sister slept on a sofa in the tiny living room. Such extremely intimate surroundings were not uncommon in families of similar background and limited financial means.

Sally's physical health, other than the usual childhood illnesses, was normal. The only exception was a serious fall from a tree at age six. Although x-rays at the time revealed no permanent damage to her head, this fall would be mentioned again in an interview between my grandfather and a United States Probation Officer days before his sentencing. My grandfather continued to question whether that childhood accident had somehow precipitated what he understood as the strange "mental malady" which led to Sally's eventual diagnosis.

My mother mentioned during one of our conversations that Sally was simply "different" than other kids, that she had few friends, and that the majority of her time she was a typical tag-along-sister. The Jewish community in Cheyenne was small and everyone seemed to know about, and care about, everyone else. When a group of children played in the street, the mother living nearest to the commotion was the de facto parent in charge. People looked after each other, one benefit of living in small-town America. In most cases, such closeness also meant everyone knew everyone else's business.

Sally's most distinguishing physical feature was a complexion a shade darker than her parents, her four siblings, and her classmates. For this never-explained departure from the norm, Sally, according to my mother, was given the cruel nickname "Blackie," a slur that followed her all the days of her pathetically short life. In telephone interviews with three of her former classmates, Sally's nickname, "Blackie," was always mentioned, along with recollections of her being extremely shy. When I gaze at the one Levin family photo still in existence, Sally does look different from the others. It's not a stretch to imagine this young girl taunted by bullies and braggarts, hiding out when she could, or seeking the protection of a sympathetic brother or sister whenever possible. I can only envision Sally as she appears before me today: slightly darker than the others, petite in stature, and square chinned—a look of quiet resignation in her ten-year-old eyes. It is likely that Sally Levin already understood, even at this tender age, the pain that being different often engenders.

It would seem that normalcy prevailed in Sally's life until she entered her teens. It's not known at what point her behavior began to change or exactly when the family became complicit in concealing her condition to the outside world. In early July of 1937, with the entire family at home, Sally turned on the gas stove in the house. In another incident, she brandished a knife one night intent on stabbing herself and one of her brothers. It was these two events that escalated Sally's situation to ominous heights and forced my grandfather to admit the seriousness of his daughter's condition. Sally was a danger to herself and others, including the rest of the Levin family. The time had come to go beyond the confines of their own front door and seek medical advice.

Based on the report of her two attempted suicides, a family physician, Dr. Bunton of Cheyenne, diagnosed Sally as suffering from dementia praecox[1], what in today's psychiatric nomenclature we know as schizophrenia[2]. As previously mentioned, Dr. Bunton suggested my grandfather seek a second opinion in Denver, knowing that it would take the signatures of two physicians to have Sally committed. There, the original diagnosis was confirmed: Sally's illness was incurable and she was an imminent risk to herself and others. The die had been cast and my grandfather knew it.

On the long ride back to Cheyenne, it's possible that father and daughter discussed the fact that Sally would soon be uprooted from all she knew and forced to live out the remainder of her life far from home. For a young girl who had rarely left her small town, the thought of going to Evanston, located in the remote southwest corner of the state, must have been overwhelming, to say the least. Was it at this point that Sally told her father she would rather die than go to Evanston?

In 2004, when I first began researching the many pieces of this puzzle, I knew there were only two people still alive who knew the details surrounding Sally's story: my mother and my uncle. I had already spoken with my mother, and she had reluctantly shared a few morsels of information about her sister, but we both knew she was holding back. On my annual visit home that year, a family brunch was planned and I thought this would be the perfect opportunity to ask questions about my long deceased relative. As we were all leaving the restaurant that morning, I turned to my uncle, Sally's younger brother, and asked if he would be willing to talk with me about his sister.

"Uncle," I said as I casually linked my arm through his. "I'm going to write a book about Sally. I'd like to interview you since you were the youngest child in the family and probably remember the most about her and what happened the day she died (he was 15 at the time). If it would make things any easier," I babbled on, "I could fly back to California one day soon and we could do the interview in person—just you and me."

Silence.

My uncle stopped in his tracks and dropped his arm, leaving mine dangling awkwardly in mid-air. He turned to me, and in a voice that was ice-cold and laced with anger, he muttered under his breath, "Don't ask me about Sally again. I will *never* discuss her. Not now and not ever!"

At that moment, my worst suspicions were confirmed. There was a lot more to this story than I would probably ever know or comprehend. It was clear my mother and her siblings had forged an unwritten agreement to never tell their own children, including me, that there had been another sibling in the family, and that our much-admired grandfather had ended her young life under circumstances so bizarre as to completely baffle the mind.

Why did sixteen-year-old Sally so desperately wish to die? In her increasingly rare moments of clarity, no doubt she felt ashamed about the mysterious illness that distorted her reality and brought immense sorrow and confusion to the family she loved. Was it hopelessness about her condition, coupled with the fear of moving so far away from those she held most dear, that convinced Sally that death was a better alternative than life? Like many other facets of this story, we will never know for sure.

Court records indicate Sally did not exhibit any unusual behaviors before July 1937, but there may have been clues that went unnoticed along the way. If there had been incidents prior to the day Sally tried to set the house on fire, for example, then perhaps my grandfather had enlisted other family members to monitor Sally whenever possible. In some instances, a single episode marks the onset of schizophrenia, but it's more likely that Sally had behaved strangely well before that fateful summer. I do recall my mother telling me, on more than one occasion, that it was her job to "protect" Sally and that she felt a tremendous burden of guilt for not being in Cheyenne on the day her sister died. My question then and now is the same: protect Sally from what? Or protect her from whom? One thing is certain, in that tiny house, in that small, closed society, it would have been extremely difficult to hide a secret of this magnitude for very long.

Mental illness has always carried with it an enormous stigma. Across all walks of life, such a diagnosis was thought to be one of the greatest tragedies a family could endure. That sentiment was certainly true in the Jewish community in 1937. Perhaps that's why my grandfather's rabbi marginalized the diagnosis of "mental maladies" among Jews when he stated before a United States Probation Officer that " . . . insanity seldom occurs in Jewish families, and is considered a very great misfortune." Of course, that statement is inaccurate, for such illnesses know no class, gender, or religious boundaries. There is little doubt that Sally Levin's diagnosis, steeped in mystery and confusion, was deemed a disgrace to her family and her community. There was, and is still today, little sympathy and less understanding of the devastating nature of schizophrenia and other brain disorders.

On the subject of sympathy and schizophrenia, author E. Fuller Torrey, M.D. (*Surviving Schizophrenia*, HarperCollins, 1983) states,

Sympathy for those afflicted with schizophrenia is sparse because it is difficult to put oneself in the place of the sufferer. The whole disease process is mysterious, foreign, and frightening to most people. . . .

Dr. Torrey continues by saying:

Schizophrenia, then, is not like a flood, where one can imagine all one's possessions being washed away. Nor like a cancer, where one can imagine a slowly growing tumor, relentlessly spreading from organ to organ and squeezing life from your body. No, schizophrenia is madness. Those who are afflicted act bizarrely, say strange things, withdraw from us, and may even try to hurt us. They are not the same person— they are *mad!* We don't understand why they say what they say and do what they do. We don't understand the disease process. Rather than a steadily growing tumor, which we can understand, it is as if the person has lost control of his/her brain. How can we sympathize with a person who is possessed by unknown and unseen forces? How can we sympathize with a madman or a madwoman?

Today, Sally rests in the Jewish cemetery, not far from the only home she ever knew. Cars, oblivious to the eternal sleep of the dead, whiz by on busy Pershing Avenue. Planes from Warren Air Force Base, the very place where her young life so dramatically ended, soar in the clouds above. It was Sally's wish that she never leave Cheyenne and indeed, she never will. Sally's name and memory have been lost to the world for generations. It is time to tell her story, for she deserves no less.

Notes:

1. Dementia praecox (a "premature dementia" or "precocious madness") refers to a chronic, deteriorating psychotic disorder characterized by rapid cognitive disintegration, usually beginning in the late teens or early adulthood.... The primary disturbance in dementia praecox was said to be not one of mood, but of thinking or cognition. Cognitive disintegration refers to a disruption in cognitive or mental functioning such as in attention, memory, and goal-directed behavior. . . . From the outset, dementia praecox was viewed by (German psychiatrist Dr. Emil) Kraepelin as a progressively deteriorating disease from which no one recovered. The three terms that Kraepelin used to refer to the end state of the disease were *"Verblödung"* (deterioration), *Schwachsinn* (mental weakness) or *Defekt* (defect). Although "dementia" is part of the name of the disease, Kraepelin did not intend it to be similar to senile dementia and rarely used this term to refer to the end state of the disease. However, by

1913, and more explicitly by 1920, Kraepelin admitted that although there seemed to be a residual cognitive defect in most cases, the prognosis was not as uniformly dire as he had stated in the 1890s. Still, he regarded it as a specific disease concept that implied incurable, inexplicable madness. (Wikipedia, http://en.wikipedia.org/wiki/Dementia_praecox)

2. Schizophrenia is a mental illness that interferes with a person's ability to think clearly, manage emotions, make decisions and relate to others. Most people with schizophrenia have hallucinations and delusions, meaning they hear or see things that aren't there and believe things that are not real or true. Organizing one's thinking, performing complex memory tasks and keeping several ideas in mind at one time may be difficult for people who live with the illness. (The National Alliance on Mental Illness, NAMI)

Family Photo - Date Unknown

FIVE

"Mercy Slayer"

"Levin Pleads Guilty"

–The Wyoming Eagle, November 16, 1937

I was born and raised in Southern California, 30 miles from the glitz and glamour of Hollywood make-believe. When I was very young, I saw my grandfather and my grandmother almost every day. By the time I entered elementary school, my mother was working full time, so my after-school routine often included stopping by their nearby apartment for a quick hello and a handful of raspberry candies from their ever-present "sweets bowl" before heading home. Conversation was practically nonexistent on those visits, but I didn't mind. My grandfather's strong arms provided me with a safe haven from the typical torments and trials of childhood.

I don't remember my grandfather ever mentioning his life in Russia or Wyoming and I never thought to ask him. It also didn't occur to me to question the scar on his cheek or wonder why his last name differed from that of his sons. In later years, it was explained to me that, for business purposes and convenience, many first generation Americans changed or shortened their foreign-sounding names. My father and my mother's brothers did just that, distancing themselves even further from their Cheyenne, Wyoming roots—an identity I now know they may have preferred to forget.

To look at him, Sam Levin appeared quite ordinary. He was not a tall man, possibly 5′8″ and with a head as smooth as a baby's backside. As a joke, many people, including customers at the liquor store where he worked, called him "Curly." He took this good-natured teasing in stride, but I'm told he rarely cracked a smile in response.

Our family moved to a different side of town when I started junior high school, and from that time forward I only saw my grandparents when they came to our house every Tuesday night for dinner. With his head hanging low over the plate, my grandfather would attack his meal with gusto. My mother would often say, "Dad, slow down, you need to be more sociable." His reply never varied: "Esther, did you invite me over to talk or to eat." Sam Levin was just that kind of no-nonsense guy.

As far as my mother was concerned, Sam was the best of the best, the champion of the family and her obvious favorite. My mother always spoke fondly of fishing excursions with her dad and how much she cherished that special time with him, never mentioning the kid sister who often insisted on tagging along. She also told me that on frigid winter mornings, as violent snowstorms pelted their flimsily built windows with a fury too loud to ignore, her father would battle the elements to bring warm doughnuts home for the family's breakfast. This meager meal was eagerly devoured as they all sat shivering around the potbellied stove, the only source of heat in their home. To my mother, Sam Levin was a hero in many ways.

My grandfather was my mother's emotional anchor through a turbulent childhood and I doubt she ever abandoned him, even in the bleakest days after Sally died. My mother admired and respected her father above all men, for he was the rock of their family—strong, dependable and loving. My grandmother was the polar opposite—a fearful, possibly unstable woman living out her days totally devoid of expression. Exhibiting little emotion or interest in me, the imprint of her life on mine is sketchy. The faraway look in her vacant eyes was a constant as she sat beside her favorite window, frantically fanning herself in the summer or covering and recovering herself with an old shawl in the winter.

Each week of my childhood, when we gathered around my mother's beautifully set dinner table, my grandmother would invariably remove the cutlery from her place setting and methodically wipe each piece with the hem of her dress. I never remember my grandmother answering the door, dialing a telephone number, or writing her name. To my mother's credit, she never said one word about these idiosyncrasies, but rather seemed resigned to such odd behaviors—as if she had witnessed them all her life. The only time I ever recall my mother criticizing my grandmother was when she told me that, as a teenager, she was too embarrassed to invite friends over because her mother "never kept a tidy house."

To better understand Sam Levin and the decision he made to take the life of his child, one must have a sense of where he came from and the many obstacles he overcame before he found himself in the unlikely environs of Cheyenne, Wyoming.

Samuel Levin was born in Imperialist Russia on June 6, 1889. A child of the *shtetl* (a Yiddish word meaning small village), he grew up with little on his plate and fear in his heart, knowing that life, for a Jew, held untold dangers. By the time he reached manhood, young Sam had channeled the power of his fears into dreams of something better. He knew that to improve his life he had to leave Russia; it would be his only escape from an otherwise miserable existence. Once he held America in his sights, little else mattered. Along with 2 million other Jews in Russia, Sam made the necessary preparations to leave his family and the country of his birth behind.

Life for Russian Jews has never been easy. Beginning in 1791, all Jewish citizens were forced to move to an area of the country called the Pale of Settlement, a large landmass covering approximately 20% of Imperial Russia. The Pale was created by Empress Catherine the Great to limit the competition of Jewish businesses in Moscow and minimize opportunities for Jewish "evil" to impact the general population across the country.

For those living within the borders of the Pale, laws that regulated Jewish life often changed from generation to generation and from ruler to ruler. For example, in some provinces Jews with special permits, or high levels of education, were sometimes allowed to live and work in the larger cities such as Kiev and Minsk. Most Jewish citizens, however, lived in the *shtetls* which surrounded these more prosperous towns, and their well-being depended, almost entirely, on the whims and edicts of both local and national government. In the year 1885, it was estimated over 4 million Jews lived within the boundaries of the Pale. By 1891, eight years before Sam was born, 22,000 Jews were deported from Russia, many of them in chains. The noose was growing ever tighter around the Jews of Russia, foretelling a great exodus that was about to occur.

Life in the Pale of Settlement was precarious at best, wrought with extreme poverty and danger. Sam grew up in one of the many small villages *(shtetls)* that fed into the grand city of Kiev. Information about his parents, siblings, and the actual place of his birth has been lost in time. Sam may have served in the Tsar's army, as conscription of Jewish males was the law (it was voluntary for non-Jews). As soldiers, Jewish males suffered constant discrimination, persecution, and in some cases, forced conversion to the Eastern Orthodox religion. Some parents, knowing what awaited their sons, resorted to such extreme measures as shooting off a foot or amputating a number of toes in order to keep their child out of the army.

One of the most terrifying aspects of Jewish life in the Pale was the periodic pogrom, a large-scale, targeted, and repeated anti-Semitic riot wherein property was destroyed and people were harassed, injured, or killed. This type of violence began in Russia in 1821 and continued off and on until 1906. Jews were often blamed for disasters that befell the country. Anything, including a deteriorating economic climate, factory shutdowns, a shortage of jobs, and even the death of a tsar could set off a tidal wave of anti-Semitic activity across the land. It was relatively easy to blame the Jews. After all, there were millions of them and they were conveniently gathered in one area of the country. Russian Jews made easy, classic scapegoats.

Between 1903 and 1906, the pogroms became more violent. In 1903, the *New York Times* (April 28, 1903) reported on the first of two such riots that took place in the city of Kishinev, which lies within the province of Bessarabia (modern day Moldova):

> There was a well laid-out plan for the general massacre of Jews on the day following the Orthodox Easter. The mob was led by priests, and the general cry, "Kill the Jews," was taken up all over the city, The Jews were taken wholly unaware and were slaughtered like sheep. . . . The scenes of horror attending this massacre are beyond description. Babies were literally torn to pieces by the frenzied and bloodthirsty mob. The local police made no attempt to check the reign of terror. At sunset the streets were piled with corpses and wounded. Those who could make their escape fled in terror, and the city is now practically deserted of Jews.

Such incidents were frequent throughout the Pale of Settlement, especially in the province of Ukraine, which is where my grandfather and his family lived. Because pogroms were generally sanctioned by the central government and carried out by the local government, it was extremely dangerous to offer any resistance. As a direct result of the unrest in the Pale, and the general anti-Semitic climate across Russia, Jews began emigrating in staggering numbers to the United States, Israel, South Africa, and various other countries within Western Europe.

It was not uncommon for young men of Sam's age to emigrate first, save a reasonable amount of money, then send for a wife or other family members to follow, sometimes one sibling or parent at a time.

In Sam's case, he left behind his entire family in 1911, including his pregnant wife Ida—my grandmother. Their first child, a daughter, was born in Russia that same year, just months after my grandfather left for America.

Legend has it that my grandfather walked all the way to Bremen, Germany, a considerable accomplishment given that Kiev is located 956 miles from that port city. Whether truth or exaggeration he, along with thousands other determined hopefuls, had to wait in Bremen for an international Jewish charity to arrange a suitable departure date. Sam was 21 years old in 1911 when, after many anxiety-filled weeks of waiting, he finally boarded a ship headed for Galveston, Texas in search of his new life. I have tried to locate the name of the ship my grandfather sailed on, but to no avail. The name "Levin" does not appear on any passenger manifesto from Bremen to Galveston in that year. That is most likely because my grandfather's actual name was not Levin. It was common for immigration agents to misspell or completely change a newly arrived immigrant's name to one he could more easily pronounce or write.

The primary support for Jews seeking passage out of Eastern Europe was HIAS, the Hebrew Immigrant Aid Society. This organization, which began in 1881, would eventually help over 100,000 Jews settle in America. By 1907, the immigrant situation in New York was threatening to explode. In an effort to divert the flow of Eastern European immigrants away from New York City's crowded lower east side and other east coast cities, The Galveston Movement was born. Several Jewish organizations in the United State and Europe, and individual philanthropists, supported the Galveston Movement.

Rabbi Henry Cohen, writing for the *The Jewish Herald* (Houston, Texas) on November 12, 1908, stated that:

> The so-called Galveston movement to divert Jewish immigration from New York to the gulf port has attracted wide attention. The doubt has been as to the feasibility of the plan. . . . The plan has been effective for (such) a short time that sufficient data to answer the question positively have not yet accumulated. Still the experience of one of the most important distribution centers for the Galveston movement is instructive. Of approximately 1,000 immigrants who landed in Galveston in the six months following the establishing of the Jewish Immigrants Information Bureau, July 1, 1907, about 10 per cent, were sent to Kansas City, where they came under the care of the United Jewish Charities and of Jacob Billikopf, superintendent.
>
> An individual record of each of these hundred persons has been kept by him. It was rarely necessary to furnish board longer than a week at an individual cost of between five and six dollars. Within that time positions were almost invariably found. The period covered includes the months of financial depression which made employment uncertain. Mr. Billikopf found 375 jobs for his hundred charges. In most instances positions were lost through no fault of the employees. Rarely have more than half a dozen men been out of work at one time, for the West has not been so seriously affected by the financial depressions as the East.

All sorts of occupations are represented among the immigrants. There are tailors, shoemakers, bricklayers, tinners, blacksmiths, butchers, bookkeepers, locksmiths, woodworkers. Wherever possible the men have been provided with work at their own occupations. In many cases, however, this has proved impossible and they have taken whatever offered. At present the tailors are making the highest wages. In some instances their pay has gone to $17 and $18 and even $20 a week. Of the eighty-eight persons listed as at work May 1, forty-eight were receiving wages under $10 a week, with $5.50 as the minimum. Thirty-six were getting between $10 and $15, and four were making $15 or more, the maximum being $20.

The record kept at the office of the United Jewish Charities in Kansas City makes interesting reading. There is W. B., for instance, soapmaker, who arrived July 1, 1907. He is working in a packing house for $9 a week. Since his arrival he has saved $175 and has sent for his family in Russia. N. P., a tailor who is making $16 a week, has saved $100 and expects to send for his family. I. Z., a laborer in a junk yard at $9 a week, has sent more than $100 to Russia. M. G., who arrived August 6, out of his salary of $10.50 a week as a sash and door maker, has saved $100 and has sent for his oldest daughter from Russia. M. B., an iron worker, on $12 a week saved $110, and now has taken a small farm.

So it goes down the list, with only two discouraging entries—one man who was implicated in a theft and left town, and another who is listed as an undesirable citizen, working only occasionally. But fourteen of the immigrants, working for the most part at meager wages, are credited with having saved $1,265 since their arrival in Kansas City. . . .

As it is, they (the immigrants) are rapidly being transformed into Americans. The great social service of the organized Jewish charities in this transformation process is self-evident. If these Russian Jews, ignorant of the language and with their low standard of living, were plumped down into the West—into Kansas City, for instance—with no one to look after them, they would starve for a few days and then would drift into the ranks of unskilled labor, with the chances against their ever rising. With the aid of the Charity Organization Society they are able to start above the poverty level. So they have a chance to look about with a view to improving their condition. First they see the need of learning English. This is provided for by the night schools of the Jewish organization—which ought to be supplanted by public night schools. And then they begin to look for a better job.

The Texas State Historical Association also contains information about The Galveston Movement:

The members of the first group (of immigrants who arrived in Galveston in July, 1907) were distributed among cities and communities throughout the western states and as far north as Fargo, North Dakota. The main territory to which the bureau directed immigrants was between the Mississippi

River and the Rocky Mountains.... Recruiters stipulated that immigrants should be able-bodied laborers and skilled workers under the age of forty.... In 1909 a total of 773 immigrants arrived in Galveston, and the following year 2,500 had sailed to the port. In 1911 (the year my grandfather emigrated) some 1,400 arrived, only 2 percent of the total Jewish immigration to the United States in that year.... Between 1907 and 1914, when it ceased operation, the Jewish Immigrants' Information Bureau brought 10,000 immigrants through Galveston, approximately one-third of those who migrated to the Holy Land during the same period.

It is unknown how or why my grandfather chose to begin his new life in Omaha, Nebraska. Perhaps it chose him. Considering Sam Levin was most likely penniless and alone in the world, he probably arrived by train under the guidance of one of the Jewish agencies responsible for immigrant placement. Omaha would have made sense under the terms of The Galveston Movement, since its goal was to place newly arrived young men in the interior of the country. The following year, 1912, my grandmother came to America with her young daughter in tow and family life began in earnest. Two more children were subsequently born in Omaha, my mother and an older brother. With three children and a wife to care for, my grandfather worked for two years at Swift and Company as a meat packer and then for two more years with the Union Pacific Railroad. In 1915, learning free land was available in Wyoming via The Enlarged Homestead Act of 1907, the Levin family packed up and headed west. For the second time in his life, Sam Levin went in search of something better and never looked back.

Signed into law by President Abraham Lincoln on May 20, 1862, the original Homestead Act allowed individuals the opportunity to work, and eventually own, 160 acres of undeveloped federal land west of the Mississippi River. The requirements for ownership were few: the applicant had to be 21 or older, live on the homestead for five years, and show evidence of having made improvements to the land.

By the time my grandfather arrived in Granite Canon (Canyon), Wyoming to begin his new life as a homesteader, most of the prime farming land in the western states had already been claimed. To encourage people like my grandfather to take up homesteading on what was essentially dry land, suitable only for ranching, the U.S. government increased the available acreage to 640 per individual. For Sam Levin, a Jewish man denied the right to own land in his native country of Russia, the opportunity to own land in America must have been exhilarating.

" . . . There is no doubt the concept of free land was both an attractive and desirable objective. Positive images associated with working and owning land meant the possible realization of the yeoman heritage idealized in popular and classical literature. For immigrants, land ownership was a symbol of wealth heretofore denied them." ("Jews in Wyoming," Carl V. Hallberg, Wyoming Council for the Humanities)

The word "Wyoming" is Dakota Indian for "large plains," and Granite Canon was the perfect embodiment of this definition: a vast expanse of land suitable only for grazing livestock. If Sam did reside with his family in Granite Canon while working his claim, it is possible he changed his mind in very short order. This isolated area was unfit for family life—immigrant or otherwise. Sam, however, was not deterred. He intended to fulfill the terms of the claim, but he knew it wouldn't be easy. Young, strong and determined, Sam was willing to do whatever was required to achieve his vision of the Great American Dream.

"Granite Canon (Canyon) started as a tent town at the end of the railroad as so many towns did. The Union Pacific tracks reached the area west of Cheyenne where the grade started to go sharply upward . . . Little is known of the early town of Granite Canon. There were the usual saloons, a general merchandise store and a few others. The surrounding area . . . is a beautiful setting of rolling hills and valleys. It is an ideal ranch area and ranching has always been the main industry." (Jean Bastian, Editor, *History of Laramie County*)

Because Granite Canon lies 16 miles west of Cheyenne, and by all accounts was virtually uninhabitable, especially in the dead of winter, it is presumed the Levin family lived in town, perhaps behind a small second-hand store my grandfather was able to rent. During the week, it is thought my grandfather continued his job with the Union Pacific Railroad and sold used furniture whenever possible. Then on the weekends, under the terms of the Homestead Act, Sam, traveling by hand-car (also known as a pump trolley) to his Granite Canon site, worked to improve the unforgiving land. In 1919, my grandfather leased his property to the Warren Livestock Company of Wyoming for an undisclosed amount. Four years later, in 1923, he sold his entire claim to Warren Livestock for the grand sum of $1 and unnamed goods.

.My grandfather was an ordinary man who loved America and appreciated the sanctuary it offered. He also believed a good life could be his as a result of hard work. To that end, he became a respected businessman in Cheyenne, always with an eye to improving his family's situation. The family struggled, but eventually money from the lease of his land, and savings from his job with the Union Pacific Railroad, allowed him to purchase two small houses in Cheyenne. One of these properties was used for rental income, the other for his family to live in. The houses were purchased in 1920, and my mother remembers the day they moved into their first real home as one of the happiest of her entire life.

The family settled in and soon after daughter Sally, the youngest girl, was born. Two short years later (1922), the Levin family welcomed a baby boy into their fold. This son was the last of the children born to my grandparents; their family was complete. It's unclear when Sam's employment with the Union Pacific Railroad ended and he became the full-time proprietor of his used furniture store. With the growth of his family, Sam's position in the Jewish community also continued to rise. He was active in his synagogue and served as president of the Jewish Council the year before Sally's death. Sam Levin had come a long way from the desperate conditions of his Russian youth. A naturalized citizen with a home, family, and business of his own, Sam, despite the ravages of The Great Depression, was living a life beyond anything he could have imagined back in Russia.

No. 703050

CERTIFICATE OF CITIZENSHIP — Number 330

Petition, Volume 3

Description of holder: Age 29 years; height 5 feet, 6 inches; color, white; complexion, dark; color of eyes, brown; color of hair, black; visible distinguishing marks, None.

Name, age and place of residence of wife Ida Levin; 28 years; Granite Canon, Wyoming.

Names, ages and places of residence of minor children Mary, 6 years; Asker, 4 years; Esther, 2 years; (All residing at Granite Canon, Wyoming.)

United States of America,   } S.S.
District of Wyoming.   }

It is remembered that

(Signature of holder.)

Sam Levin

Naturalization Certificate
—*Wyoming State Archives*

Be it remembered that

—— Sam Levin ——

then residing at ——— , in the
—— of ——— Granite Canon ——— State
—— Territory of ——— Wyoming ———

—his naturalization was a subject of ——— Russia ———
did make application to be admitted a
citizen of the United States of America pursuant to law, and, at a —— regular ——— term of the ——— District
Court of —— United States ——— held at —— Cheyenne, Wyoming, on the — 1st — day of — July ———
in the year of our Lord nineteen hundred and —— eighteen ——— the court having found that the petitioner had resided con-
tinuously within the United States for at least five years and in the —— State ——— for at least one year immediately preceding the
date of the filing of his petition, and that said petitioner intends to reside permanently in the United States; had, in all
respects complied with the law in relation thereto, and that —he was entitled to be so admitted, it was thereupon
ordered by the said court that —he be admitted as a citizen of the United States of America.

In testimony whereof the seal of said court is hereunto affixed on the —— 1st ——— day of —— July ———
in the year of our Lord nineteen hundred and —— eighteen ——— and of our Independence the
one hundred and —— forty-second. ———

Clerk U.S. District
Court U.S. District Wyo
By _____ Bradley _____ Deputy

Naturalization Certificate
–Wyoming State Archives

258

LAND PATENT RECORD

No. 12034?

THE S. A. BRISTOL CO., PRINTERS AND BINDERS, CHEYENNE

LAND PATENT

TO

THE UNITED STATES

Sam Lewin

CHEYENNE 020124

THE STATE OF WYOMING, } ss.
County of Laramie,

This Instrument was filed for record on the 30 day of October......, A. D. 19.20., at 10:30 o'clock .... A. M., and is duly recorded in Book 219 on Page 258..... *Wa. R. Graham*

County Clerk and ex officio Register of Deeds

By .... Deputy

THE UNITED STATES OF AMERICA,

To all to whom these presents shall come, Greeting:

WHEREAS, a CERTIFICATE OF THE REGISTER OF THE LAND OFFICE at Cheyenne, Wyoming, has been deposited in the General Land Office, whereby it appears that, pursuant to the Act of Congress of May 20, 1862, "TO SECURE HOMESTEADS TO ACTUAL SETTLERS ON THE PUBLIC DOMAIN," and the acts supplemental thereto, the claim of *Sam Lewin*

Land Patent Record
—Wyoming State Archives

.... has been established and duly consummated, in conformity to

law, for the *west half of*

.... of Section *twelve*

Township *twelve* .... north of Range *fifty-nine* .... west of the Sixth Principal Meridian, Wyoming, containing *three hundred twenty acres*, ... acres, according to the OFFICIAL PLAT of the Survey of the said Land, returned to the GENERAL LAND OFFICE by the Surveyor General:

Now KNOW YE, that there is, therefore, granted by the United States unto the said claimant .... the tract of land above described: To HAVE AND TO HOLD the said tract of Land, with the appurtenances thereof, unto the said claimant .... and to the heirs and assigns of the said claimant .... FOREVER; subject to any vested and accrued water rights for mining, agricultural, manufacturing, or other purposes, and rights to ditches and reservoirs used in connection with such water rights,

Land Patent Record
–*Wyoming State Archives*

as may be recognized and acknowledged by the local customs, laws, and decisions of Courts, and there is reserved from the lands hereby granted, a right of way thereon for ditches or canals constructed by the authority of the United States.

In Testimony Whereof, I, *Woodrow Wilson*

President of the United States of America, have caused these letters to be made patent; and the seal of the General Land Office to be hereunto affixed.

Given under my hand, at the City of Washington, *in District of Columbia* the *Twenty first second* day of *September* nine hundred and *twenty* , in the year of our Lord one thousand , and of the Independence of the United States the one hundred and *forty-fifth*

L. J. C. Lawson
.... Recorder of the General Land Office

By the President: *Woodrow Wilson*

By *M. P. Le Roy* , Secretary

Recorded: Patent Number *774378*

Land Patent Record
—Wyoming State Archives

WARRANTY DEED

WARRANTY DEED

Sarah Lewis
Jane Lewis

TO

The Harrow Live Stock
Company

THIS DEED, Made this .... day of .... and twenty-third between ...... Sarah Lewis and Jane Lewis ....

.... part.... of the first part, and ....

The Harrow Live Stock Company, a Wyoming Corporation

.... part .... of the second part;

WITNESSETH, That the said part.... of the first part, for and in consideration of the sum of ...... One dollar ($1.00) and other good and valuable consideration .... Dollars, to .... them .... in hand paid by the said part .... of the second part, the receipt whereof is hereby confessed and acknowledged, ha.... granted, bargained, sold and conveyed, ... and by these presents do .... grant, bargain, sell and convey .... unto .... said part .... of the second part, and unto .... its .... heirs and assigns, forever, all .... that piece .... or parcel of land, situate, lying and being in the County of Laramie and .... State of Wyoming, and more particularly known and described as follows, to-wit:

The State of Wyoming, } ss.
County of Laramie.

This Deed .... was filed for record at .. 3 .... o'clock
.... P.M., on the ...... 10 .... day of ...... July .... ,
A. D. 19.25 ., and .... duly recorded in Book 251 on Page 21.

P.P. ....
County Clerk and ex-officio Register of Deeds.

By .... Deputy

.... in the year of our Lord One Thousand
Nine Hundred .... and twenty-third .... between ...... Sarah Lewis and Jane Lewis ....

Warranty Deed
—*Wyoming State Government*

The West half of Section Twelve (12)
Township Thirty-nine North, Range
Sixty-nine (69) West, the 6th P.M.
Laramie County, Wyoming.

Warranty Deed
—Wyoming State Government

And the said part .... of the first part hereby expressly waive ... and release ... any and all right... benefit... privilege... advantage... and exemption... under and by virtue of any and all statutes of the State of Wyoming, providing for the exemption of homesteads from sale on execution or otherwise.

To Have and to Hold the said above described .... premises unto the said part.... of the second part, ... heirs and assigns of the first part, for .... forever; together with the privileges, hereditaments and appurtenances thereunto in any wise appertaining or belonging. And the said part.... .... of the second part, ... heirs, executors and .... administrators, do.......... covenant and agree to and with the said part.... of the first part, ... well seized in the said premises, in and of a good and indefeasible estate in fee simple.

And that they are free from all incumbrances whatsoever ....

And that they ... hereby ... good and lawful right to sell and convey the same. And the said part.... of the first part will, and .... heirs, executors and administration shall Warrant and Defend the same against all lawful claims and demands whatso...

And the said part.... of the first part, for ..... of the second part, ... heirs, executors and administrators, do covenant and agree to and with the said part.... of the second part, ... heirs and assigns, that .... the said part.... of the second part, shall and may lawfully as at all times hereafter, peaceably and quietly have, occupy, possess and enjoy the said p...

Warranty Deed
—Wyoming State Government

SIX

The Far Away Place

"I Am Going to Do This Because I Don't Want to Go to Evanston"
–*The Wyoming Tribune*, August 8, 1937

Sally Levin was determined to die.

In the month before Sally Levin was diagnosed with the "mental malady" known as dementia praecox (schizophrenia), we know she attempted to take her own life on at least two separate occasions. Soon after two physicians declared her legally insane, the date of Sally's commitment to the Wyoming State Hospital in Evanston (often referred to simply as "Evanston") was set. According to court records Sally, lost within the mire of a madness she could neither comprehend nor control, begged her father to end her life. When my grandfather initially refused to comply with her bizarre request, the distraught teen then urged him to die alongside her. Sally, as with so many others who suffer from major mental illnesses, was intent on ending her life, one way or another.

The rate of suicide attempts and completions is staggering among schizophrenics. As reported on schizophrenia.com (http://www.schizophrenia.com/szfacts.htm):

> People with the condition have a 50 times higher risk of attempting suicide than the general population; the risk of suicide is very serious in people with schizophrenia. Suicide is the number one cause of premature death among people with schizophrenia, with an estimated 10 percent to 13 percent killing themselves and approximately 40% attempting suicide at least once (and as much as 60% of males attempting suicide). The extreme depression and psychoses that can result due to lack of treatment are the usual causes. These suicide rates can be compared to the general population, which is somewhere around 0.01%. (Source: *Treatment Advocacy Center* and other sources)

It should not be overlooked that while there is no official record of what happened while she was hospitalized in Denver, Sally may have witnessed, or experienced for herself, such frightening moments during her brief stay that the thought of dying paled before the specter of life within an insane asylum. Psychiatry was in its infancy in the 1930s and there were few options open to someone with her illness. For Sally, age 16, it was either commitment to Evanston, possibly for life, or remain a virtual prisoner at home under lock and key.

Schizophrenia has been with us since the beginning of recorded time. In ancient Greece, the philosopher Plato defined two types of madness: a revered and respected madness believed derived from divine origin, and the more garden variety madness generally feared and reviled by the populace. In this same time period, Jewish scholars attributed the term "divine madness" to the prophets in the Hebrew Bible. Through the ages, individuals who heard voices, experienced hallucinations, or showed other outward signs of abnormality were often labeled mystics, saints, or emissaries of the Devil.

In the Middle Ages, and especially in Europe, people who exhibited strange or unusual behaviors were often considered possessed. Little distinction was made between those who were mentally retarded, physically disabled, or mentally ill. An individual labeled as "possessed" might, at least initially, be exposed to calming music in an attempt to soothe his or her troubled mind. For more extreme cases, exorcism, generally administered through the Church, was standard practice. If that failed to produce the desired effect, holes might be drilled into the sufferer's head to clear a pathway for evil thoughts to escape the body. As in colonial times, the label "witch" was frequently given not just to those believed possessed by the Devil, but also to those who refused to tow the majority line regarding government policy or religious doctrine.

In Colonial America, the mentally ill considered most docile were often allowed to wander about at will, while more violent individuals were imprisoned and forced to endure an array of cruel punishments that included bleeding, ice baths, shackles, and solitary confinement. It is interesting to note that the mentally ill of this time were often referred to as "lunatics" because it was thought they were born under the spell of a full moon.

In the 19th Century, thanks to the extraordinary efforts of social reformer Dorothea Dix, numerous insane asylums were built in the United States. It was during this period that an array of groundbreaking treatments for the mentally ill emerged: some good, many very bad.

In the asylums, many experimental methods of treatment were tried... Dr. Benjamin Rush, sometimes called the father of American psychiatry, was the first president of the American Psychiatric Association and his face still appears on the official seal. In 1818, Dr. Rush (one of the signers of the Declaration of Independence) and the most renowned doctor of his time, wrote, "Terror acts powerfully upon the body through the medium of the mind and should be employed in the cure of madness. Fear accompanied with pain and the sense of shame has sometimes cured the disease." Dr. Rush advocated and practiced terror by designing and using the straitjacket, the tranquilizer chair, and "fear of death" on numerous inmates in 19th century lunatic asylums. . . .

. . . Despite some of his more bizarre cures, Rush is admired for being one of the first to believe that mental illness was a disease of the mind, rather than a possession of demons. Rush forced the hospital to cease its policy of chaining the most serious cases of the mentally ill in unheated basement cells despite the common belief that the insane could not feel hot or cold. And he (also) stopped the practice of letting the townspeople come to the hospital to watch the insane patients as a form of entertainment.

("History of Treatments of Schizophrenia and Other Madness,"
schizophreniatreatments.bravehost.com/history.html)

In 1887, newspaper reporter Nellie Bly, from the *New York World*,
managed to convince numerous physicians and a judge that she was
hopelessly insane. Working undercover for her newspaper, Bly was
committed to the Women's Lunatic Asylum on Blackwell's Island
(New York). For ten days, Bly observed asylum conditions firsthand
and later published her book, *Ten Days in a Madhouse*. This tell-all
book received critical acclaim and an outpouring of citizen rage
that shocked the nation. Her exposé resulted in improved conditions at New York state asylums, including more careful diagnosis
of individuals considered insane.

Ms. Bly wrote, "The food consisted of gruel broth, spoiled beef,
bread that was little more than dried dough, and dirty undrinkable
water. The dangerous patients were tied together with ropes. The
patients were made to sit for much of each day on hard benches with
scant protection from the cold. Waste was all around the eating places.
Rats crawled all around the hospital. The bath water was frigid, and
buckets of it were poured over their heads. The nurses were obnoxious
and abusive, telling the patients to shut up, and beating them if they
did not." (http://en.wikipedia.org/wiki/Nellie Bly)

The use of hydrotherapy also gained popularity in the 19th century
and would have been a procedure used at Evanston in the 1930s:

This treatment consisted of several devices and tech-
niques that made use of water. The two most popular means

of administering hydrotherapy were the continuous bath and the wet sheet pack. Following a doctor's order for a "pack" (since it was a medical intervention, a doctor's order was always required), an attendant would dip a sheet in water ranging from 40 to 100 degrees Fahrenheit, then snugly wrap it around the patient and tie the patient to the bed . . . Patients remained in this cocoon-like state for several hours. At first, the individual might experience cooling as water evaporated off the dripping, water-soaked cloth but, as his or her body began to generate heat, the pack would warm . . . By the 1910s, most psychiatric institutions in the United States were using hydrotherapy . . . ("History of Treatments of Schizophrenia and Other Madness," http://www.schizophreniatreatments.bravehost.com/history.html)

Looking back upon the decade of the 30s, Sally's decade of death, medical historians now acknowledge that many treatments designed to improve patient care were cruel and, in some instances, deadly. Perhaps the most controversial procedure practiced in this era was the lobotomy, an intervention Sally most likely would have been forced to endure.

The original lobotomy was a medical procedure where the neural passages from the front of the brain are surgically separated from those in the back of the brain. The common result of this procedure was the patient forgetting their depressing or discouraging feelings or tendencies. This was a very delicate, time-consuming procedure that required great skill and training from the practicing surgeons. . . .

The most famous lobotomist was a physician named John Freeman. It is thought Dr. Freeman, known as "the traveling lobotomist," operated on at least 3,000 patients diagnosed with schizophrenia. . . . Due to the number of complications and deaths that resulted from the procedure, it was referred to as "psychic mercy killing" and "euthanasia of the mind." This was by far mental health care's darkest hour. (Kimberly Leupo, "The History of Mental Illness," http://www.toddlertime.com/advocacy/hospitals/Asylum/history-asylum.htm)

In 1886, the Wyoming Territorial Assembly appropriated funds to build the Wyoming Insane Asylum in Evanston at a cost not to exceed $30,000. Construction began in 1888 and doors opened to Wyoming's "idiots, lunatics, and insane persons" the following year. Prior to this time, mental patients from Wyoming were transported to Illinois or Iowa for treatment. In 1897, the name of the asylum was changed to Wyoming State Hospital for the Insane. In 1923, the name was changed again, this time to the Wyoming State Hospital. Today, the facility still exists as the Wyoming State Hospital, and it is the only psychiatric hospital in the state. Several of the original buildings on the campus remain and have been designated historical landmarks.

The Wyoming asylum couldn't have been more remote, a brick and mortar testimony to the lonely, isolated life mental patients often experienced. The town of Evanston is located in the southwest corner of the state and its growth depended almost entirely on oil and the building of the transcontinental railway by the Union Pacific Railroad. The climate in and around Evanston is dry and the altitude is high at 6,748 feet above sea level, making this mental hospital the highest and one of the most isolated in the United States. It was here that Sally Levin would have spent her young life, perhaps her entire life, nearly 400 miles from the only home she had ever known.

One of the first patients at the Wyoming asylum was E. T. Payton. A well-known newspaperman and author of two books, *Mad Men* and *Behind the Scenes at Evanston*, Payton wrote about his frequent stays at the asylum. Payton told of patients "choked and beaten" by the hospital's attendants. He also described a beating he endured and his time in solitary confinement. He once claimed the colors of the institution were "black and blue." (Rick Ewig, "E. T. Payton: Savior or Madman?" *Annals of Wyoming*, Vol. 79, No. 1)

In 1932, five years before Sally would have been committed to Evanston, the superintendent of that institution, D. B. Williams, M.D., wrote his biennial report to the Wyoming Board of Charities and Reform. Below are several excerpts from that document.

Within (its) doors, the emphasis was placed in making each day attractive. Daily papers were distributed to the wards, and there were always plenty of magazines to read, and during the summer season, flowers and plants were provided to the wards, as well as the dining rooms.

Everything happens to our patients that can happen in any town of five hundred people. All of the various physical ailments are taken care of, as well as the mental, and frequently there is surgical work of an emergency nature. A great many of our patients are old and helpless and require bed attention. . . . Ward rounds are made twice daily and orders for treatment are written by doctors in charge. . . . There are no special accommodations for epileptic patients, although we receive several each year. Hydrotherapy is carried out on all disturbed cases, either sedative or stimulative in nature. The hydrotherapy department was moved to the disturbed wards where it was needed. ("Board of Charities and Reform: Wyoming State Hospital," *Biennial Report*, 1932)

Dr. Williams' narrative continues:

Various kinds of entertainment are provided, and the patients look forward to these events. As we do not have talking moving pictures, our patients are taken to the theater in Evanston, which we are able to rent for an afternoon at a reasonable rate. The patients' library is used to good purpose, but most of the books are now old and worn.

The Wyoming State Hospital is glad to report that very little restraint is used at this time. The only restraint permitted is for the purpose of preventing a patient from mutilating himself or doing great harm to someone else, which is the case with two patients now on the ward for the criminal insane. ("Board of Charities and Reform: Wyoming State Hospital," *Biennial Report*, 1932)

At the time the above information was submitted, the staff at the Wyoming State Hospital included: 1 superintendent (a physician), 1 assistant physician, 1 business manager, 3 nurses, 32 other nurses and attendants, and 14 other officers and employees. This was for a patient population of 305 males and 210 females. The average age of female patients was 49.95 years old. The average age of male patients was 50.05. Dr. Williams further noted there were 90 deaths during the biennial period. The greatest number of patients died from general paralysis and exhaustion from chronic mental disease, followed closely by deaths resulting from cerebral hemorrhage and bronchial pneumonia. ("Board of Charities and Reform: Wyoming State Hospital," *Biennial Report*, 1932) It is clear that Sally, age 16, would have been alone and without a peer group among the older population at Evanston.

In 1937, in the midst of the Great Depression and massive budget cuts at every level of government, it is likely that Dorothea Dix's ideal of humane treatment for patients had devolved into some level of custodial care at Wyoming's only psychiatric hospital. After years of searching for answers about conditions at the hospital in the year 1937, it has been discovered that such information simply does not exist. In fact, it is quite remarkable that the superintendent reports about the Wyoming State Hospital from 1933 through 1950 have somehow disappeared. Without documentation, one is left to speculate as to what may or may not have happened in that faraway place.

"Unfortunately, for our understanding of the Wyoming State Hospital during this period, critical records are missing. None of the biennial superintendents' reports from 1933 through 1950 are extant in the Wyoming State Archives, the State Library, or the University of Wyoming." (Barbara Bogart, "The Hospital on the Hill," *Annals of Wyoming, Winter 2007*).

Although Wyoming State Hospital's biennial reports during the years Sally would have lived at the institution are unavailable to review, it may be enlightening to learn about conditions in similar facilities for the mentally ill. There was a journalist, Albert Q. Maisel, who wrote a scathing exposé about mental health care in the United States just seven years after Sally would have begun her life at the asylum in Evanston. In his extensive article, written for *Life Magazine* and entitled "Bedlam 1946," Maisel stated, "most U.S. mental hospitals are a disgrace." As in the time of Nellie Bly's book, *Ten Days in a Madhouse*, Maisel's investigative report also outraged a national audience. In it, the author described horrific conditions in state mental hospitals in Cleveland, Ohio and Philadelphia, Pennsylvania, and indicated that similar practices existed in hundreds of state-run institutions across the country. In part, Maisel wrote:

> In Philadelphia the sovereign Commonwealth of Pennsylvania maintains a dilapidated, overcrowded, undermanned mental "hospital" known as the "dungeon." One can still read, after nine years, the five-word legend, "George was killed here, 1937."
>
> This pitiful memorial might apply quite as well to hundreds of other Georges in mental institutions in almost every state in the Union, for Pennsylvania is not unique. Through public neglect and legislative penny-pinching, state after state has allowed its institutions for the care and cure of the mentally

sick to degenerate into little more than concentration camps on the Belsen (notorious Nazi concentration camp) pattern.

Court and grand-jury records document scores of deaths of patients following beatings by attendants. Hundreds of instances of abuse, falling just short of manslaughter, are similarly documented. And reliable evidence, from hospital after hospital, indicates that these are but a tiny fraction of the beatings that occur, day after day, only to be covered up by a tacit conspiracy of mutually protective silence and a code that ostracizes employees who sing too loud.

Yet beatings and murders are hardly the most significant of the indignities we have heaped upon most of the 400,000 guiltless patient-prisoners of over 180 state mental institutions.

We feed thousands a starvation diet, often dragged further below the low-budget standard by the withdrawal of the best food for the staff dining rooms. We jam-pack men, women and sometimes even children into hundred-year-old firetraps in wards so crowded that the floors cannot be seen between the rickety cots, while thousands more sleep on ticks, on blankets, or on the bare floors. We give them little and shoddy clothing at best. Hundreds—of my own knowledge and sight—spend twenty-four hours a day in stark and filthy nakedness. Those who are well enough to work slave away in many institutions for 12 hours a day, often without a day's rest for years on end. One man at Cleveland, Ohio—and he is no isolated exception—worked in this fashion for 19 solid years on a diet the poorest sharecropper would spurn. . . .

. . . Worst of all, for these wards of society we provide physicians, nurses and attendants in numbers far below even the minimum standards set by state rules. Institutions that would be seriously unmanned even if not overcrowded find themselves swamped with 30%, 50% and even 100% more patients than they were built to hold. These are not wartime conditions but have existed for decades. Restraints, seclusion and constant drugging of patients become essential in wards where one attendant must herd as many as 400 mentally deranged charges. (Albert Q. Maisel, "Most U.S. Mental Hospitals Are a Shame and a Disgrace," http://www.pbs.org/wgbh/americanexperience/features/primary-resources/lobotomist-bedlam-1946/)

Did scenarios, similar to those described by Maisel, also exist in Wyoming's only public mental health institution? Without official confirmation to the contrary, it is difficult to say. It is possible that the compassionate conditions at Evanston described in Dr. Williams' glowing 1932 report continued through the decades. It seems there were asylums in the United States that, even with limited resources, managed to provide competent patient care. I would like to believe the Wyoming State Hospital at Evanston might have been one such place. We will never know for sure. One thing is certain, Sally Levin had no intention of ever finding out.

Wyoming State Hospital

—Courtesy of Evanston Public Library

Wyoming State Hospital
—Courtesy of Evanston Public Library

Wyoming State Hospital

–Courtesy of Evanston Public Library

SEVEN

In The Name of Justice

"I Am Not Afraid"
–The Wyoming Eagle, November 18, 1937

On August 16, 1937, the major news story of the day concerned defending the international city of Shanghai against the Empire of Japan's superior military might. As the world turned its collective eye toward aiding an overpowered and outmatched China, the citizens of Cheyenne, Wyoming struggled to understand another story of gigantic proportion much closer to home.

In Wyoming, the rough and tumble "cowboy" state famous for its great expanse of barren land and Native American heritage, the residents of Cheyenne learned that a heinous crime had been committed in their city. This crime, so unfathomable, so disturbing, would remain a talking point among townspeople for years to come. Exactly three months and one day after my grandfather shot and killed his daughter, a final verdict was rendered in Criminal Case #4267. The controversy surrounding his crime, however, was far from over.

Some believed the sentencing my grandfather received was fair, given the extenuating circumstances involved in this most unusual case. Others felt that a more severe punishment was warranted, and that my grandfather literally got away with murder. There was speculation that Sam Levin's suspended sentence, and permission to complete his probation in another state, was influenced by prominent members of the Jewish community in Cheyenne anxious to have my grandfather leave town as soon as possible—taking his shame and disgrace with him.

By today's standards the justice system, at least in my grandfather's case, moved swiftly toward its dramatic conclusion. It had initially been reported in the local press that Sally's shooting took place within the city limits of Cheyenne and the case, therefore, would be tried in Laramie County. However, on August 20, 1937, it was learned Sally's murder had, in fact, been committed on federal property. The following day, August 21, 1937, the citizens of Cheyenne awoke to this headline and article in *The Wyoming Eagle*:

"U.S. PROBES LEVIN CASE" AND "SLAYING TOOK PLACE UPON RESERVATION."

Federal agents today will launch an investigation into Sally Levin's death, following the discovery yesterday that Sam Levin ... fatally wounded his daughter within the boundaries of the Ft. Warren military reservation.

The department of justice probe was instigated after undersheriff E. D. Brown and a post official examined the scene ...

west of C & S track embankment halfway between Highway 30 and Happy Jack Road.

The shooting occurred from 50–75 feet within the boundary of the military post (Fort Warren military reservation).

At the conclusion of his examination, Brown notified U.S. District Attorney Carl Sackett, who in turn advised the Department of Justice at Denver. . . .

. . . What weight action taken here by the coroner's jury which ruled Levin insane and not to be held responsible for the slaying would have in the government investigation could not be determined yesterday.

With Brown's disclosure the possibility appeared for the first time that Levin may have to stand trial on murder charges.

The result of this newest twist in an already baffling story meant that the state of Wyoming, represented by County and Prosecuting Attorney Caldwell, was forced to withdraw from my grandfather's case since it was now under federal jurisdiction.

On August 24, 1937, eight days after Sally's death, the much anticipated sanity hearing took place in Cheyenne. The findings from that hearing, preceded by the following paragraph, were reported in *The Wyoming Eagle* the next day (August 25, 1937):

"The federal government will file murder charges against Sam Levin following a report of the Laramie county sanity commission yesterday that found the 48-year-old merchant sane, John C. Pickett, assistant U.S. district attorney said last night."

The newspaper article continued with details from the hearing:

> This is to certify that we have this day examined Mr. Sam Levin now at Memorial Hospital to determine if he is mentally incompetent on the present date.
>
> The result of our examination is as follows:
>
> There is no evidence at this time of any unusual mental reactions, such as delusions, hallucinations of any type, mental depression or excitability.
>
> He (Sam Levin) states clearly to us what he did at the time of the shooting and gives his reasons, but admits that he did wrong in killing his daughter and attempting to take his own life, and that he would not do those things in his present frame of mind.
>
> We, therefore, on the basis of the above findings, feel Mr. Sam Levin is mentally competent at present time and shows no evidence of insanity.

My grandfather knew that had he been found insane at this hearing, he would have been sent immediately to the insane asylum at Evanston, the very place thought to be the catalyst for the murder-suicide attempt in the first place.

According to the Wyoming Revised Statutes of 1931, the definition of an insane individual is "any person, who by reason of unsoundness of mind is incapable of managing his own estate, or is dangerous to himself or others if permitted to go at large, or is in such condition of mind and body as to be a fit subject for care and treatment in a hospital for the insane. No person mentally defective from birth, or whose mental development was arrested by disease or physical injury occurring prior to the age of puberty, and no person who is afflicted with simple epilepsy is regarded as insane, unless the manifestations of excitability, violence, or homicidal or suicidal impulses are such as to render his detention in a hospital for the insane a proper precaution."

The following day, August 25, 1937, charges of voluntary manslaughter were filed in federal court against my grandfather. This crime carried a maximum penalty of ten years in prison. Federal officers and my grandfather's attorney, C.A.Swainson, were present at the hospital when the warrant and complaint were served. It was reported that my grandfather showed little emotion at the time and that, after a nod from his attorney, he waived examination. After several men from the Jewish community posted a $10,000 bond (double what was normally required in such cases), my grandfather was released from custody and allowed to return home.

As the citizens of Cheyenne enjoyed fall's blessed relief from the blistering summer of 1937, the Levin family knew these cooler days meant their long wait was nearing its end. They prepared themselves for the next step on the road to my grandfather's eventual sentencing: a hearing and verdict by the federal grand jury. In a statement to *The Wyoming Eagle* (November 9, 1937), my grandfather was quoted as saying, " 'I am not afraid. Whatever the jury feels it must do will be all right. What already has happened has hurt me so much that nothing now can hurt me more deeply. It is hard to tell you how I feel, but my future doesn't mean much to me now.' "

Grand juries rarely fail to indict in capital offenses. Therefore, when the verdict rendered in Criminal Case # 4267 on November 8, 1937, was announced, few people in the town of Cheyenne were surprised:

IN THE DISTRICT COURT OF THE UNITED STATES FOR THE

DISTRICT OF WYOMING.

UNITED STATES OF AMERICA)
)
)
(
vs. (
(NO. ___4267___ CRIM.
SAMUEL LEVIN. (
)
)
(

INDICTMENT for violation of Section 453,
Title 18, USCA. Manslaughter
committed within limits of a
Military Reservation.

A TRUE BILL:

_____
Foreman of Grand Jury.

CARL L. SACKETT,
United States Attorney for the
District of Wyoming.

JOHN C. PICKETT,
Asst. United States Attorney for
the District of Wyoming.

Grand Jury Verdict, Cover Page
—*The National Archives, Federal Records Center*

UNITED STATES OF AMERICA) SS.
DISTRICT OF WYOMING.)

In the District Court of the United States for the Dis-
trict of Wyoming, said district being a part of and within the
Tenth Judicial Circuit of the United States, at a regular term of
said District Court begun and held at the City of Cheyenne, in the
County of Laramie and State of Wyoming, in the District of
Wyoming and Judicial Circuit aforesaid, on the eighth day of
November, in the year of Our Lord one thousand nine hundred and
thirty-seven:

The Grand Jurors of the United States of America, good
and lawful men, summoned from the body of said District of Wyoming
within said Tenth Judicial Circuit of the United States, then and
there being, and then and there being duly impaneled, sworn and
charged by the Court aforesaid, to diligently inquire and true
presentment make for said District of Wyoming, in the name and by
the authority of the United States, upon their oaths do find,
charge and present:

That heretofore, towit, on the sixteenth day of August,
in the year of Our Lord one thousand nine hundred and thirty-seve
at a point or place located within the limits of that certain
Military Reservation known as the Fort Francis E. Warren Military
Reservation, a place then and there within the exclusive jurisdict
of the United States of America, in the County of Laramie, in the
District of Wyoming, within the boundaries of the State of Wyoming
within said Tenth Judicial Circuit, and within the jurisdiction of
this Court, one SAMUEL LEVIN, then and there being, did wilfully,
knowingly, unlawfully and feloniously, without malice, and in a
sudden heat of passion and in the commission of an unlawful act,

Grand Jury Verdict, Page 1
—The National Archives, Federal Records Center

make an assault in and upon one Sally Levin with a deadly weapon,
commonly called a gun, the same being then and there charged and
loaded with gunpowder and bullets, and then and there being held in
the hands of the said SAMUEL LEVIN, and the said SAMUEL LEVIN
did then and there feloniously, wilfully, knowingly and unlawfully,
without malice, and in a sudden heat of passion and in the
commission of an unlawful act, point at, discharge and fire at,
against and upon the said Sally Levin the said bullets so
discharged and fired from said gun, and did thereby mortally
wound the said Sally Levin in such a manner that the said Sally
Levin died a short time thereafter; and the said SAMUEL LEVIN,
in the manner aforesaid, did then and there wilfully, knowingly,
unlawfully and feloniously KILL the said Sally Levin, contrary
to the form of the statute in such case made and provided, and against
the peace and dignity of the United States of America.

United States Attorney for the
District of Wyoming.

Confident there would be enough evidence to justify an indictment of manslaughter by the grand jury, it had already been determined that my grandfather was a viable candidate for probation. President Herbert Hoover signed the Federal Probation Act, a relatively new judicial option, into law in 1925. This piece of legislation gave the U.S. Courts power to appoint Federal Probation Officers and the authority to sentence appropriate defendants to probation, rather than prison terms. It is interesting to note that the interview below was conducted on November 7, 1937, the day before the grand jury convened. The information in this document would prove crucial in my grandfather's sentencing.

UNITED STATES DISTRICT COURT

OFFICE OF PROBATION OFFICER

DISTRICT OF WYOMING

REPORT OF U. S. PROBATION OFFICER

FILED

NOV 17 1937

Charles J. Ohahaus
Clerk

LEVIN, Samuel, Crim. #4267.

CHARGE: Manslaughter.

SOCIAL HISTORY	Your Probation Officer visited Levin Sunday, November 7, 1937, and talked with him alone.
	Age 48. Born in Russia. Entered the United States at Galveston, Texas, 1911. Came to Wyoming in 1916. Naturalized in 1920 at Cheyenne.
	Educated in the Hebrew schools in Russia.
FAMILY	Married Ida in Russia in 1909. Children are: Mary, daughter, born in Russia, 27, married, in Los Angeles Archie, son, lives in Los Angeles Esther, daughter, 22, employed as bookkeeper Sally, " 16 Max, son, 17, in high school.
	Mary, Archie and Esther graduated from Cheyenne high school, Archie had one year in the University of Wyoming.
WORK RECORD	In Omaha, worked 2½ years for Swift & Company Work 2½ years for Union Pacific Railroad Co. Came to Cheyenne, 1916, and worked for U. P. 5 years. In the meantime took up a homestead 16 miles southwest of Cheyenne, and then engaged in the furniture business up to the present.
RELIGION	Jewish. Was last year President of the Jewish Council in Cheyenne.
MILITARY SERVICE	Registered for the World War but was not called.
RESOURCES	In addition to the store, until recently owned two houses, 1901 and 1905 East 20th Street.
PHYSICAL CONDITION	Family have enjoyed good health with the exception of Sally who experienced a physical and mental break about July 1, 1937.
INSTANT CASE	Probation Officer visited Levin in his home and he gave in substance the following statement regarding this trouble:

Probation Report, Page 1

–The National Archives, Federal Records Center

The beginning of Sally's mental turn occurred about July 1st.
They felt it was both a physical and mental break. She had had a
serious fall when she was about six years old, and the parents took
her to Dr. Day for physical examination. They insisted on an X-ray,
and Dr. Day took her to the Burton clinic, but the X-ray failed to
show any difficulty.

Dr. Bunten diagnosed the present case as dementia praecox, and
stated that she would not likely improve. It was suggested that
they take her to Dr. Hilton, a specialist in Denver, who corroborated
Dr. Bunten's diagnosis. Her condition by this time had grown more
serious, so they placed her in a private sanitarium in Denver where
she remained one week. They then brought her home.

Levin states that Sally was in a great mental disturbance over the
fact that they felt she would never be well again, and made several
attempts to take her own life, once by turning on the gas, and second
with a butcher knife.

Papers were then made out for her commitment to Evanston, to which
she protested and begged her father to end her life rather than put
her away. Levin stated that in in his disturbed condition over her
he had a feeling that perhaps he was going the same way, and this
feeling grew in intensity. Sally finally proposed that if he would
not put her out of the way that he go with her. The time had come
for the completion of the papers for her commitment and go to Dr.
Shingle for his signature. He claims he was without sleep for a
week or ten days, and when Sally protested against going to Evanston,
and insisted on the compact to end her life, Levin agreed, and
instead of going to Dr. Shingle, drove to the edge of town where
the deed was committed.

Levin states that when he came to and found himself in the hospital
on a cot beside the cot on which Sally lay and heard the doctor
announce that she was dead, that he experienced a sense of relief
that he did not know how to described, and which he was sure if
he did, noe one would understand. He had carried out her desires
and his only disappointment was that he had failed in his attempt
to go with her.

This story as given to the Probation Officer corroborates in all
important particulars the facts brought out at the coroner's inquest.

Probation Officer also contacted Mrs. Levin who states that her
husband has always been a kind, gentle man, fond of his family,
that he talked little but kept his troubles to himself.

Probation Officer contacted Esther, who corroborated her mother's
statement that her father was always kind to his family and very
fond of all his children.

Levin, Samuel, Crim. #4267. concluded.

Contact was also had with Rabbi Krasch, who came to the Probation
Office and discussed the case. Rabbi Krasch explained that Levin
had been President of the Jewish Council the past year, and had
enjoyed a good reputation among the Jews. The Rabbi was on his
vacation when this tragedy occurred, and states that he believes
if he had been here, in his extremity Levin would have come to
him and he would have been diverted from carrying out his decision.

Rabbi Krasch stated that insanity seldom occurre in Jewish families,
and is considered a very great misfortune.

NOT
PSYCHO-
PATHIC

Only one other instance that could be in any way significant
was discovered in the Levin family; that of the oldest daughters
marriage to a gentile sometime ago. Levin was greatly disturbed
over it. According to Rabbi Krasch, he felt that a marriage
outside of the fold was a reflection upon the family and that
her family could never be accepted into the Jewish households.
He was very critical of Mary, to the extent that he in turn
was severely criticized by other members of the Jewish
congregation.

Probation Officer asked Dr. Andrew Bunten if he felt that the
emotional flare expressed at the time of Mary's marriage had any
connection with this disturbance in the way of a general psycho-
pathetic condition or a diseased mind. Dr. Bunten stated that he
did not believe there was any connection between the two, that each
instance grew out of the circumstances surrounding these two
matters.

Dr. Bunten further states he did not believe Levin would be psycho-
pathetic and that he did not believe there is any danger of a
repetition of a trouble of this sort. He based his statement on
the attitude of Levin immediately after the tragedy. He stated
that in a psychopathic condition would have found Levin highly
emotional, whereas in this instance he seemed calm and resigned.

U. S. Probation Officer

On November 15, 1937, Sam Levin was arraigned before Federal Judge T. Blake Kennedy. According to *The Wyoming Eagle* (November 16, 1937), "He (Sam Levin) waived reading of the charges against him and when asked for his plea, replied in a low voice, 'Guilty.'" The judge deferred sentencing until November 17 and the family went home to wait.

At 10 a.m. on November 17, 1937, my grandfather, Sam Levin, sat in a packed and hushed courtroom and learned the consequences of his actions. In considering the defendant's application for probation, one can easily discern Judge Kennedy's thoughtful and compassionate response in the pages that follow:

IN THE DISTRICT COURT OF THE UNITED STATES
FOR THE DISTRICT OF WYOMING.
———————

UNITED STATES)
)
    v.   )   No. 4267 Crim.
)
SAMUEL LEVIN.)

By the Court on Application for Probation.

The case now before the Court is of a strange paradoxical nature and therefore the more difficult to dispose of. It can probably be most aptly described as one which is sometimes called
"Mercy homicide." There are those who openly espouse the legitimacy of such a method of ending human suffering. No doubt most
people are strenuously opposed to it. A goodly number may be in
doubt when the most favorable circumstances lend strength to its
humane purpose. Perhaps no one would favor an indiscriminate rat-
ification of the aim based solely upon the mental operation of the
agent who seeks to accomplish the desired end in the relief of the
afflicted. Certainly all would agree that "carte blanche" justification of this type of homicide would be exceedingly dangerous.

It is beyond the province of the Court I take it, in a time
like the present to attempt a philosophical discussion and a determination of the correct answer to the question.

In this case there has been an indictment returned by a Grand
Jury which charges this defendant with the crime of manslaughter.
The finding of this body is exclusively within its own province.
If one should feel that the charge should have been murder in the
first degree it is no answer here. In the ordinary understanding
the charge of manslaughter means the taking of human life with a

Judgment on Application for Probation, Page 1
—*The National Archives, Federal Records Center*

degree of mitigation, but without complete justification. The Grand Jury therefore must have felt that the crime revealed to them had elements which partook of a form of mitigation or quasi-justification. At least all that we have before us is an indictment for manslaughter to which the defendant has entered a plea of guilty and has presented application for Probation.

The term probation is comparatively new in the jurisprudence of the Federal courts and is perhaps generally somewhat misunderstood. It is not essentially intended to be made applicable to the crime committed but more especially to the person who commits the crime. Its objective is restitution and reconstruction of character in the individual whose background, temperament, previous conduct, and moral and economic sense of responsibility seem to justify it. Hence we see those entering pleas of guilty to the same class of crime treated differently; some being favored with probation and others committed to institutions. This must be the rule or else the Probation System would be but a farce. And whenever it is seen that probation is not indulged when applied for in good faith, it certainly means that that individual has developed in the investigating and administering officers no hope for reconstructed character either on account of previous misconduct or mental and moral irresponsibility. Frequently by straining our hope without the ordinary background, we are met with disappointment and defeat and sometimes our best judgment is shockingly upset.

On account of the serious nature of the crime in the instant case, the matter has been investigated with more than the usual care by the proper officials, to bring forward all points which bear upon this particular feature of the case. As the picture has been presented to me, the defendant is or was the father of a family consisting of both boys and girls. One of these, a girl aged about 16 years, became afflicted with a disease which thorough research, competent investigation and adequate treatment was thought to be both incurable and progressive. The daughter was aware of her condition and implored the father to end her suffering and what to her was felt to be a disgrace. This so preyed upon the father's mind that the only way out seemed to be the mutual ending of their double misery in a joint death. This was attempted by the defendant with a successful result as to the child, but with a serious but not mortal wound as to the father. At least it can be said that he himself tried to keep the faith. But he is now here to answer to the almost unforgivable offense of having slain his own offspring.

His life up to the time of that overwhelming crises had been normal so far as investigation reveals; a good husband; a natural and loving father; a good business-man; a man who paid his honest debts; one who took pride in the rearing and equipping of his children with an adequate education; one respected by his fellow-citizens and by those of his class and association, recognized by being placed in positions of responsibility, respect and honor. Being of the Jewish faith, it may be said with at least a degree of plausibility that this great sorrow which so strangely entered into his life found its expression in the strong family ties predominating this proud race.

If the picture be painted without the absolute character of the crime itself, the background is as perfect for the indulgence of a probation plea as one could well find. Does this element destroy it? No man can answer that question with a degree of certainty. Minds differ as they depend upon many varying phases of physiological reactions. Certain it is that no system of administrative criminal justice should condone the act here charged or ratify its commission. Nor does this Court. But in the philosophy of the Probation theory, this would not appear an insurmountable obstacle.

With one who was so obessed with the love for his child that
he himself would lay down his own life with hers, it can scarcely
be said that he is devoid of the sensibilities of life; that he is
possessed of genuine criminal instincts; or that there is in him a
remote degree of danger of future lawlessness along this or other
lines.   This then must be the measure of the Court's judgment,
against whose fallibility there is no insurance,in this as in all
human affairs.

The sentence and judgment of the Court is that the defendant
be committed to an institution to be designated by the Attorney
General for a period of five years, but that the sentence be suspended and the defendant be placed on probation with the duly designated Probation Officer of this Judicial District for a period
of five years.

All that was left on that morning was the reading of Judge Kennedy's Sentence and Judgment Under Probation Act, the document that outlined the terms of my grandfather's probation. This final chapter of Sam Levin's judicial journey is presented in the pages that follow:

IN THE DISTRICT COURT OF THE UNITED STATES

FOR THE DISTRICT OF WYOMING

-o-

UNITED STATES OF AMERICA,)
                Plaintiff,)
)
       vs.   )   No. 4267 - Crim.
)
SAMUEL LEVIN,   )
               Defendant.)

SENTENCE AND JUDGMENT UNDER PROBATION ACT.

At this day comes Carl L. Sackett, Esquire, District
Attorney, who prosecutes the pleas of the United States in this behalf, and the defendant, Samuel Levin, in his own proper person and
by Clarence A. Swainson, Esquire, his attorney, also comes.

The defendant, Samuel Levin, having been indicted and arraigned and having plead "Guilty" to the crime of manslaughter committed
within limits of a Military Reservation, in violation of Section 453,
Title 18, U.S.C.A., is then asked by the Court if he has anything to
say why the sentence and the judgment of the Court should not be
pronounced against him, to which the defendant replies that he has
and thereupon makes a statement to the Court.

IT IS THEREFORE CONSIDERED, ORDERED AND ADJUDGED by the
Court that the said Samuel Levin be committed to the custody of the
Attorney General of the United States, or his authorized representa-
tive, to be confined in an Institution for the period of five (5)
years from this date, but it appearing to the Court that it would be
proper in the premises to place said defendant on probation, under
the Act of March 4, 1925, for the period of said sentence, IT IS
HEREBY ORDERED that said defendant be, and he is hereby, placed on
probation for said period of five (5) years, or during good behavior,
under the care and custody of Joseph B. Lutz, United States Probation
Officer, Cheyenne, Wyoming, and that during such probation period he
shall comply with the general conditions of probation as fixed by the
Attorney General of the United States, said defendant to remain at all
times subject to the jurisdiction of the Court under the provisions

Sentence and Judgement, Page 1
–The National Archives, Federal Records Center

of said statute.

IT IS FURTHER ORDERED that a certified copy hereof be delivered to the said United States Probation Officer.

Dated this 17th day of November, A. D. 1937.

_____ Judge.

It was over. On the morning of Thursday, November 18, 1937, the first photo of my grandfather appeared in *The Wyoming Eagle* with the caption "I Feel Better Today Than I Did Yesterday."

Eagle Photo and Engraving

"I Feel Better Today than I did yesterday." Thus did Sam Levin express himself yesterday morning after Federal Judge T. Blake Kennedy placed him on probation for the mercy slaying of his 16-year-old daughter, Sally. Mrs. Levin said she was pretty happy also. The 48-year-old furniture dealer is shown here in the first picture ever taken of him for publication.   Photo by Francis Brammar

–The Wyoming Eagle, November 18, 1937

"'I am very grateful for the understanding accorded me,'" Levin said after sentencing was pronounced in a courtroom almost filled with spectators.

The article also stated "He (Sam) is contemplating sale of his furniture business here and moving to another city to establish a store. However, he has not decided definitely upon such a move . . . His daughter, Esther (my mother), embraced him as they left the courtroom. She cried softly while Judge Kennedy spoke on Levin's application for probation. Levin stood unmoved, but showed some emotion after sentence was pronounced." (*The Wyoming Eagle*, November 18, 1937)

When all was said and done, a devoted husband and father was not sent to prison for his unimaginable crime. A family traumatized by their loss and scarred by their shame, would soon pack up and leave town. One daughter would remain behind, alone and forgotten for generations.

EIGHT

The "Good Death"

"I Am Going to Do This Because I Don't Want to Go to Evanston"
–*The Wyoming Eagle*, November 9, 1937

It is unlikely my grandfather had ever heard the word "euthanasia," let alone knew its definition. What he did know was the Hebrew Bible and of course, the moral and ethical teachings embodied in that most sacred text: The Ten Commandments. Although the sixth commandment (in Judaism) states in no uncertain terms that "Thou Shalt Not Kill," my grandfather did kill, as have countless millions down through the ages.

Euthanasia, the "good death," is defined as "the act or practice of killing or permitting the death of hopelessly sick or injured individuals in a relatively painless way for reasons of mercy." (*Merriam-Webster Dictionary*, http://www.merriam-webster.com/dictionary/euthanasia). It is generally accepted that two types of euthanasia exist: passive euthanasia—withdrawing any treatment (i.e. medications, medical procedures) that would prolong life, and active euthanasia—actually assisting a person to die by a variety of means—including, but not limited to, lethal injections, medications, shooting, drowning, etc.

The controversy over taking one's life, or that of another's, to relieve suffering dates back to antiquity. While some Greek philosophers disdained suicide by any means, there were many who were more tolerant of its use when they deemed the situation appropriate. Perhaps the most enduring words on the subject of suicide avoidance came from the Greek physician Hippocrates in the 4th Century B.C. In his medical school, all doctors were required to take what is known as the Hippocratic Oath. This pledge, the very cornerstone of medical ethics, has stood the test of time and is still recited by doctors at medical school graduations to this day: "I will not give a deadly drug to anybody if asked for it, nor will I make a suggestion to that effect."

Among the great religions of the world—Judaism, Christianity, and Islam—suicide is forbidden. In the 13th century, St. Thomas Aquinas elaborated on the Christian argument against this act "by claiming suicide was a sin against God because only God had the right to take back the gift of life that He had given. Indeed, he wrote, suicide was the worst of sins because it left no time for repentance." (Lisa Yount, *Right to Die and Euthanasia,* Rev. ed., Infobase Publishing, 2007)

In the 18th century, famous European philosophers David Hume and Immanuel Kant espoused totally opposing views on the issue of euthanasia. Hume believed that "suicide to end a life of severe illness or disability, in which one can contribute little or nothing to society and is enduring intolerable suffering, not only is acceptable, but may even confer a net social benefit." (Lisa Yount, *Right to Die and Euthanasia,* Rev. ed., Infobase Publishing, 2007)

Offering a different perspective, Immanuel Kant, according to Ms. Yount, felt that "suicide showed disrespect for life. He (Kant) agreed with Aquinas that the act usurped a power that belonged only to God and violated one's duty as a created being." (Lisa Yount, *Right to Die and Euthanasia,* Rev. ed., Infobase Publishing, 2007)

Over the centuries, the issue of euthanasia, or "mercy killing" as it is sometimes known, was as widely debated in the United States as in Europe. Through world wars and economic depressions, the argument over an individual's right to die raged on. At the time of Sally's death, euthanasia was an illegal act in every state in the union. The right to die is still a hotly contested issue and is only legal under certain circumstances in three states today.

Following the pronouncement of Sally's death, my grandfather's initial reaction was relief that he had honored his child's wishes. That short-lived emotion turned to remorse within twenty-four hours, but by then it was too late; the damage had been done. When did the enormity of my grandfather's crime morph into a nightmare of grief and shame and when, if ever, did it dissipate?

One can only speculate as to the atmosphere in the Levin household once my grandfather returned home from the hospital after posting bond. Did the surviving children express resentment and anger over their father's deed, or were the siblings awash in relief that Sally was now, and forever, out of her misery?

It is possible that during the three months between Sally's death and my grandfather's sentencing, the Jewish community rallied around my grandmother and her surviving children, embracing them with compassion and understanding in spite of the revulsion they may have felt for my grandfather, the now infamous "mercy slayer." It is more likely the entire family suffered the same degree of rejection accorded my grandfather. Since I don't know what really happened in those anxiety-filled weeks, I am left to imagine the worst-case situation: my mother's anguished and isolated family living each interminable day under a shadow of humiliation and disgrace.

According to one newspaper report, the family's home was sold during this time period and my mother, her younger brother, and my grandparents moved into an apartment. Was this move predicated on the sentiment that my grandfather could no longer abide in the house where Sally had once lived, or was he merely preparing for his family's eventual move from Cheyenne—with or without him?

As the Jewish community reeled from the news that one of their own had committed a crime from which, for many, there would never be forgiveness, my grandfather's days were spent working in his store, providing for his family, and preparing his case with his attorney. Considering the precarious state of his reputation, it is most likely Sam Levin went out of his way to avoid interaction with the many townspeople who now held him in such low esteem. In a town as small as Cheyenne, it would be impossible for my grandfather not to notice the swirl of controversy that surrounded him at every turn.

The Jewish principle regarding the sacredness of life is central to the faith, and assisting in a suicide has never been condoned. In the words of Rabbi Richard S. Rheins of Temple Sinai (Denver, Colorado):

> The sanctity of life, *kiddushat ha-chayim*, is the cornerstone
> of Judaism and there is no sin more grievous than the taking of

another person's life. The only exceptions are in times of war, for self-defense, or in the rare cases of capital punishment, which are meted out, in Jewish law and tradition (*Halakhah*) only with extraordinary precautions.

Even hastening the death of the terminally ill is forbidden under *Halakhah*. The *Shulchan Arukh*, the great law code of Judaism, emphatically states that one who speeds the death of the terminally ill (*goses*) by means of the simplest of actions (removing a pillow or closing the eyes) is likened to one who is a murderer (*Shulchan Arukh, Yoreh Deah*, 339.1). While it is sometimes permissible to remove that which artificially delays death (*Iggerot Moshe, Yoreh Deah* 2), this is done only when death does not immediately occur after the removal.

Therefore, it is quite clear: Jewish law and ethics forbid both euthanasia and assisted suicide. But, in this sad case, the act of a father shooting and killing his mentally imbalanced daughter is not an example of euthanasia or assisted suicide. Rather, it is simply an act of premeditated murder. In no way can his action be justified as putting the troubled soul of his daughter out of her misery. The very concept of mercy killing is foreign to Judaism. No murder, much less the murder of one's own daughter, is justifiable.

My grandfather had violated a fundamental tenant of his faith not once, but twice. Taking Sally's life, and then attempting to end his own, may have wrapped the Jewish community of Cheyenne in a blanket of collective shame. Because of their historical status as a religious and often hated minority in many lands, the Jewish mindset has long been to keep a low profile whenever possible. Translation: As a Jew, do not bring *any* negative attention upon yourself or on your people which might result in criticism or trouble. The almost-daily newspaper articles about Cheyenne's "mercy slayer" did little to enhance the reputation of a predominately immigrant group of people who yearned for nothing more than to be accepted as upstanding, law-abiding citizens in their adopted homeland.

As my grandfather struggled through the rituals of daily living while awaiting the decision that would determine the rest of his life, his emotional state over Sally's death surely carried with it an indescribable degree of guilt and shame over what he had done.

Jeffrey Kauffman, editor of the book *The Shame of Death, Grief, and Trauma* (Routledge, 2010) writes in his essay entitled "On the Primacy of Shame," that " ... guilt is the feeling that 'I have done something wrong,' and shame is the feeling that 'I am something wrong.'"

Mr. Kauffman continues:

"There are many ways in which grief arouses shame . . . such as shame for being alive while the other is dead, for the inward disorder of grief, for being frightened, being vulnerable to death, being outcast, helpless, and abandoned. . . ."

The question of euthanasia, referred to in this instance as "mercy slaying" and "mercy homicide," was paramount in my grandfather's case. Although he clearly did not understand all the historical and legal controversy surrounding the subject, he knew he had committed a grave offense and that he would live with the consequences of his act for the rest of his life.

Two days after my grandfather's sentencing, when perhaps the air around him smelled a little sweeter and his heart beat a little slower, the editorial in the morning paper brought a measure of closure to a tragic event that would define a family for all time. That editorial is presented here in its entirety:

An Interesting Decision

Seldom is a court required to pass judgment in a case of more paradoxical nature or more difficult of analysis than the "mercy slaying" case which was on the docket of the federal district court in Cheyenne this week, and in which the defendant had entered a plea of "guilty."

That the decision of Judge Kennedy in which sentence was suspended and the defendant placed on probation will meet with the approval of other jurists, members of the bar and the public generally goes without saying. That the statement which accompanied the sentence and judgment of the court will be crucially studied by other jurists, and that it will establish a precedent which will influence decisions in similar cases may also be conceded. As Judge Kennedy says, the term "probation" which contemplates the "restitution and reconstruction of character in the individual" is comparatively new in the jurisprudence of federal courts.

The "highlights" of Judge Kennedy's statement are incontrovertible and when soberly considered it is easy to understand the conclusion which justified, or we might say required, the judgment rendered in this case.

"There are those who openly espouse the legitimacy of such a method of ending human suffering," said the judge, although "all would agree that 'carte blanche' justification of this type of homicide would be exceedingly dangerous. . . . Certain it is that no system of administrative criminal practice should condone the act here charged or ratify its commission. Nor does the court."

Nevertheless, although most people are opposed to "mercy slayings," many will be in doubt "when the most favorable circumstances lend strength to its humane purpose." That such a condition obtained in this case will be the verdict of all who are familiar with it. For after an investigation conducted "with more than usual care by the proper officials," it was determined that the defendant was "so obsessed with the love for his child that he himself would lay down his life with her," that he is not possessed of genuine criminal instincts; and that there is not "in him a remote degree of danger of future lawlessness along this or other lines."

Therefore, as the court well said, the background in this case is as perfect for the indulgence of a probation plea as one could well find. With which opinion other jurists will no doubt agree, although the paradoxical nature of the problem makes it most difficult to dispose of. (*The Wyoming Eagle*, November 19, 1937)

NINE

Turning Away

" 'Mercy Slayer' Given Five-Year Probation, May Leave Cheyenne"
–*The Wyoming Eagle*, November 18, 1937

My grandfather's crime, an act conceived in desperation and executed in shame, changed our family's history forever, just as he knew it would. As word of the verdict swept through Cheyenne, the Levin family made plans to flee the nest in search of greener, more forgiving pastures. My mother married her hometown sweetheart exactly four days after the trial ended and headed for California the very next day. My father, along with my mother's older brother, had purchased a package (liquor) store in the town of Lomita, California earlier that year. The oft-told story is that my parents, in an act of total rebellion against the religious constraints of their insulated world, dined on pork products at every meal on their trek westward to the Promised Land. My mother had never eaten pork before, as her family observed the dietary rules known as *Kashrut* (kosher) in which pork is a forbidden food. Arriving in Lomita on Thanksgiving Day,

1937, there was only enough money left for one meal, which was fine with my mother. Sick from an excess of ham, bacon, and pork chops, she claimed she dined on water and soda crackers, while my father enjoyed a traditional Thanksgiving dinner.

Several months after my mother passed away, I was told a poignant story that speaks to the outrage many Jews in Cheyenne felt toward the Levin family. Immediately following Sally's death and the news that my grandfather would stand trial for her murder, the rumor in the Jewish community was that my father would not marry my mother due to the shame now associated with the Levin name. This revelation could explain why my parents married so quickly after the trial and then immediately left the state.

To my knowledge, my mother visited Cheyenne only once in her lifetime after moving to California. In late July of 1968, she flew to Denver to be with me after the birth of my first son. Her one request that visit was that I drive her up to Cheyenne to spend time with her best friend from childhood days. Sensing it was important to her, I readily agreed to the trip. I learned only recently that this was the same person who, despite stern warnings from her own mother in 1937 to cross the street should she ever come face-to-face with the "mercy slayer," never abandoned my mother or our family. The two women remained close, enjoying a friendship that endured over ninety years.

My grandparents, along with their 15-year-old son, the youngest of the five Levin children, packed all they could fit into their vehicle and headed for the west coast as soon as winter break (1937) began. My uncle, a teenager at the time, was devastated to leave his friends behind, but what choice did he have? Surely the traumatic circumstances of the previous months had a huge impact on the man he later became. I don't believe this uncle ever returned to Cheyenne, and he flatly refused to discuss anything about his long-deceased sister or the events that so changed the course of his life. Even on his deathbed, he would not speak her name. My uncle was living at home that August day in 1937 when disaster struck and I believe he knew the details of Sally's death. Yet, other than a brief explanation to his new wife, he chose to keep his secrets to himself.

My mother's oldest sister, the sibling she had been visiting on the day Sally died, had eloped with a Gentile not long before Sally's passing. This unforgivable act of marriage to a non-Jew was a disastrous blow to my ultra-religious grandparents. After learning of her forbidden marriage, my grandparents sat *shiva* in her memory, an act that proclaimed her dead to the family and to the world. Considering what had happened to this family over the course of just a few short months, that first meeting in California between a distraught and grieving father and his estranged daughter must have been traumatic. Growing up, I knew nothing about this catastrophe in the Levin family and I have no knowledge of when my aunt's eventual reconciliation with my grandparents took place, only that it did. Perhaps it was in the lonely years following their exodus from Wyoming that a path was cleared to bring parent and child together again. The emotional pain of one daughter straying from the faith helps me understand, at least to some degree, how the second heartache over Sally's devastating diagnosis must have affected my grandfather's momentous decision to end both her life and his.

My grandparents settled in the town of Baldwin Park soon after their arrival in California, and my grandfather found employment as a clerk in a neighborhood liquor store. It was during these first 5 years that my grandfather was required to fulfill the terms of his probation. In doing so, he was expected to meet with the probation officer assigned to his case on a regular basis. He was also not allowed to travel outside the jurisdiction in which he lived and he could not own or carry a weapon of any kind. Because of these restrictions, it would have been impossible for my grandfather to be present when Sally's gravestone was carved or dedicated. Nobody knows who paid for the stone's creation and, strangest of all, why Sally's name was misspelled as Salie. Did the stone carver's hand slip or did the person ordering the stone simply not know the correct spelling of Sally Levin's name?

Speaking of names, "confused" might well have been mine. A lonely child, I knew at a very early age that something was missing in my life and that whatever that something was lay just beyond my grasp. I simply did not, could not, connect with my mother. When she looked at me, I thought I saw disapproval and disappointment reflected in her eyes. I felt unwelcome, a stranger in my own home. These people, I thought to myself, couldn't possibly be my real parents, for I was in no way like them. Convinced I was unwanted, the sadness of my childhood escalated into the rebellion of my youth. My sour disposition, and what I perceived as my mother's blatant disinterest in my life, left me floundering. My mother's days seemed joyless, as if she were an observer rather than a participant in everything around her. So, by default, I felt obligated to not enjoy my life either. Of course, having no inkling at the time of the horrific events that had befallen her family, I made all my assumptions based on ignorance.

After years of research on this story, I have come to the conclusion that the surviving children of Sam Levin created an unwritten pact to never mention Sally to their own children and to simply erase their sister's existence from our family's history. Was my grandfather complicit in this agreement, or did he actually instigate the plan and then insist that his children follow suit? My guess is that it was my grandfather, along with his elder son, who determined it was best to bury everything related to their lives in Cheyenne soon after they laid Sally to rest.

As the decades slipped by did all the family eventually forget about Sally? I doubt it. I'm quite certain my mother never forgot. I believe, in fact, that her sense of personal responsibility for her sister's death stayed with her until the end of her days. That the Levin family left Sally behind was one thing, for they had to leave Cheyenne in order to reclaim some semblance of their previous lives. What I cannot fathom is why only one family member, my grandfather, is thought to have visited her grave in all the many years since her death. On the day my mother and I drove from Denver back to the place that held such painful memories for her family, did thoughts of Sally ever cross her mind? Following many trips to Cheyenne while writing this story, I realized that on that summer afternoon in 1968 we were less than a mile from the cemetery where Sally is buried. It was my mother's chance to pay her respects to her long-deceased sister; she never, of course, mentioned a word.

For people seeking to begin anew, where better than the relaxed atmosphere of Southern California to assume a different identity and a new lifestyle as well. It would appear that all the Levin siblings turned away, in varying degrees, from the faith that had once bound them so tightly to each other and the community in which they grew up.

Looking back, I would venture to say that my grandfather, once the proud president of the Jewish Council of Cheyenne, also turned away from Judaism—at least for a time. I have, for example, no childhood memory of his visiting a synagogue or observing a Jewish holiday. Not ever. Was there a period, following Sally's death, when my grandfather, saddened and disgraced by the enormity of what he had done, believed himself unworthy to bow his head before the God he so revered? I wonder, also, if this once observant Jew continued to keep a kosher home, a religious observance ingrained within him since his childhood in Russia. Viewed as a vestige from the recent past, I know my mother and her siblings abandoned this practice soon after they crossed the Wyoming border on their way to their new lives.

My brother was born in 1940 and I followed soon after in 1942. My mother and father both worked, which meant we children were often left to our own devices. Knowing her total disdain for anything Jewish, I am perplexed as to why my mother enrolled us both in a Sunday school program at a nearby reform (liberal) temple near our home. My brother was expected to accompany his little sister (me) to and from this house of worship a scant six blocks away. Having no commitment to the faith of our forefathers, my brother was an early dropout from Judaism. As a result of his decision to no longer attend Sunday school, I had no choice but to follow in his ambivalent footsteps. Since there were no parental role models in our home for becoming cultural Jews, let alone religious Jews, I grew up not knowing the sacred holidays, the traditions, or the expectations of living a Jewish life. I didn't know enough at the time to be disappointed or angry with my parents for not exposing me to my religious heritage. Those feelings would come much later.

My mother's affection for her father was genuine. She would do anything for him; he need only ask. There was a brief period in my young life when my grandparents lived with us in a duplex-type arrangement. Our family of four—my mother, father, brother, and myself—occupied the much larger portion of a two-story house, while my grandparents lived in an apartment attached to the first floor of our home. It was an unusual living space, to be sure, but I do recall being happy to see my grandparents, especially my grandfather, almost daily. After moving out of our house, my grandparents rented two small apartments over the course of several years—each within walking distance of where we lived. I have very fond memories of frequent after-school and Sunday morning chats with my grandfather during those early years. Once they moved to the other side of town our time together was more infrequent. My mother's Tuesday night dinners, the only family ritual I recall with regularity, continued until I left the state for college.

Although the Levin family appeared, at least on the exterior, to thrive and prosper in California, the siblings, other than my mother's oldest sister, did not seem a particularly happy lot. It is my recollection that each sibling in his or her own way was secretive, suspicious, and highly critical of others. Although we all lived in the same city, our extended family rarely spent time together. I didn't know as a child why that was so, I assumed it was this way with all families. Now I can only surmise that being in such close proximity to each other increased the chances that buried secrets from their past might bubble to the surface, forcing parents and siblings to remember what they were trying so hard to forget. I knew there were squabbles between the siblings and sniping behind each other's back, for I heard it on many occasions. Were the members of my extended family always so difficult to get along with or did the circumstances of their collective experience with Sally's death mold them into the cantankerous adults they became? I can only speak for my own mother who, when I asked her why she often seemed so unhappy, said, "You would be unhappy, too, if you had to live with what I live with." Was she referring to her sister? I believe she was. On the night she passed away, when all secrets escape the hidden crevices of our soul, my mother called out Sally's name. It comforts me to think these two sisters have met again somewhere in another time and place.

As previously mentioned, my grandmother was distant and distracted—because of her own mental illness or the anguish of losing her child in such a bizarre manner, I cannot say. My grandfather, although not a jovial man by any means, was never unfriendly. He was quiet and thoughtful. He spoke little, answering questions, but rarely offering information. Yet, somehow I always regarded him as loving. Now, when dark thoughts of my family's tortured past reduce me to tears, I am comforted by fond memories of my grandfather's gentle touch. That's the man that I choose to remember and always will.

As a college project, I sat down with my grandfather one afternoon and asked him about his long life. I recorded his words back then, but I was young, and the questions I asked were simplistic. In our few hours together, he never complained or revealed the hardship and pain of leaving his Russian family behind, coming to America penniless and without friends or family, homesteading on land that yielded a pittance, and certainly not the death of his beloved daughter. Although my grandfather appeared stoic on the outside, who can say what turmoil festered deep within? How many nights did he dream of Sally, hear her call out his name, and recreate in vivid detail all that happened on that summer day when everything changed?

District Court of the United States

DISTRICT OF WYOMING

FILED

NOV 15 1937

Charles J. Ohabaus
Clerk

UNITED STATES OF AMERICA,

Plaintiff.	
vs.	No. 4267 Crim.
SAMUEL LEVIN,	
Defendant.	

____I____ do certify that__I__ have been retained by and appear in the above-entitled cause, for and in behalf of __Samuel Levin,__

the above-named __defendant.__

Dated this __15th__ day of __November__ , 19 37 .

Clarence A. Swanson

Cheyenne, Wyo.

(Kindly give post-office address)

USPA—FLK—7-21-33—1000—931-22

Discharge from Probation, Page 1
–The National Archives, Federal Records Center

PROBATION SYSTEM, U. S. COURTS

IN AND FOR THE

District Court of the United States

FOR THE

--------------DISTRICT OF--WYOMING---

> **FILED**
>
> **NOV 24 1942**
>
> Charles J. Ohnhaus
> Clerk

THE UNITED STATES

vs.

SAMUEL LEVIN

Division...............................

Docket No. C-rim. #4267.......

1. COMES NOW............JOSEPH B. LUTZ......................PROBATION OFFICER OF THE COURT
presenting an official report upon the conduct and attitude of probationer   SAMUEL LEVIN

2. PRAYING THAT THE COURT WILL   DISCHARGE PROBATIONER FROM FURTHER

SUPERVISION.

3. RESPECTFULLY RELATING THAT THE PROBATIONER.....Samuel Levin...............
was placed on probation by the Honorable...T. Blake Kennedy...............................
sitting in the court at.....Cheyenne, Wyoming., on the....17th.....day of.........November.................194.1937
who fixed the period of probation supervision at......five (5) years............................., and imposed the
general terms and conditions of probation theretofore adopted by the court and also imposed special conditions and terms as follows:

4. RESPECTFULLY PRESENTING PETITION FOR ACTION OF COURT FOR CAUSE AS
FOLLOWS:

(If short insert here; if lengthy write on separate sheet and attach)

That said probationer was permitted to go to California and has been under
the supervision of the Probation Officer there who states that probationer
has lived up to the requirements of the Court Order in a very satisfactory
manner.

ORDER OF COURT

Considered and ordered this.............day
of.......................194.....and ordered filed
and made a part of the records in the above
case.

....

Respectfully,

....
Probation Officer

Place Cheyenne, Wyoming..............

Date...November 21, 1942.............

Discharge from Probation, Page 2
—The National Archives, Federal Records Center

IN THE DISTRICT COURT OF THE UNITED STATES

FOR THE DISTRICT OF WYOMING

—o—

UNITED STATES OF AMERICA,

        Plaintiff,

   vs.

SAMUEL LEVIN,

        Defendant.

No. 4267 Criminal

ORDER DISCHARGING DEFENDANT FROM PROBATION

At this day comes Joseph B. Lutz, Esquire, Probation Officer for the District of Wyoming, and presents his official report on the conduct and attitude of probationer Samuel Levin, defendant herein, advising the Court that the period of probation of said defendant has expired, and that said defendant has not violated his probation and that his conduct has been reported as satisfactory.

IT IS THEREFORE ORDERED that said defendant, Samuel Levin, be, and he is hereby, discharged from such probation.

Dated this 24th day of November, A. D. 1942.

_____
                Judge

TEN

"The Secrets They Kept"

"Secrets are like stars. They blaze inside the heart and ultimately could be explosive. But there are two types of secrets. Small secrets, like small stars, will eventually burn out. With time and space they lose their importance and simply vanish. No harm done. But big secrets, like massive stars, with time and constant fear grow stronger, creating a gravitational pull that eventually ... When they get so big, they become a black hole."

–Jennifer Jabaley, *Lipstick Apology*

Sally and Sam Levin are gone, but remnants of their lives live on— still shrouded in secrets. In telling the incredible story that so profoundly shaped my family's history, I had hoped to find acceptance of our hidden past. Instead, my journey has led me back to where it all began, with more questions than answers, more heartbreak than peace of mind.

I believe all the surviving family members of the Levin family bore the shame and sorrow of what happened on August 16, 1937, for the rest of their days. How could they not? However, I can only speak with certainty as to how I feel the life-altering event of Sally's death impacted my relationship with my own mother. For as far back as I can remember, I struggled with the innate sense that something was wrong, something void of explanation, but bloated with the potential for disaster. Today I mourn those wasted years of my childhood for, although we lived in the same house, it could be said that our emotional paths rarely crossed in any meaningful way. Without understanding my mother's pain, the emotional barrier between us was set too high for me to climb.

According to Evan Imber-Black, PhD and author of the book *The Secret Life of Families* (Bantam Books, 1998), "If family members keep secrets from each other—or from the outside world—the emotional fallout can last a lifetime." Dr. Imber-Black identified the four main ways in which "family secrets shape and scar us:

* They can divide family members, permanently estranging them.
* They can discourage individuals from sharing information with anyone outside the family, inhibiting the formation of intimate relationships.
* They can freeze development at crucial points in life, preventing the growth of self and identity.
* They can lead to painful miscommunication within a family, causing unnecessary guilt and doubt."

Of all the secrets the Levin family kept hidden, the following remain the most troublesome to me:

There were five children in my mother's family. It has been confirmed that my mother was in California with her older sister at the time of Sally's death. That being said, exactly where were my two uncles and my grandmother when their lives came crashing down around them? And most importantly, why didn't any of them stop this disaster before it happened? I am haunted by the possibility that everyone, including my grandmother, knew something life-changing was about to happen and did nothing to prevent it.

On paper, my grandfather's suicide note made it clear that he had every intention of dying alongside his daughter. If that were so then why, after two gunshots to the head and two stab wounds in the chest, was my grandfather still unable to end his life? As he saw his child lying in a pool of blood before him, did trembling hands prevent an accurate aim? Or, after shooting Sally, did my grandfather change his mind? Is it possible that in a brief moment of clarity, thoughts of my grandmother and his other children caused him to reconsider his plan? At the very last minute, and for whatever reason, did my grandfather choose to live?

Why was Sally's skin so much darker than the rest of her family? And to what degree were certain family members more deeply troubled by this unexplained birth anomaly than others? Could it be that all the family members were, in fact, ashamed of their daughter and sister's complexion? My mother indicated that one sibling in particular verbally abused the girl with a constant barrage of insults. The fact that Sally's nickname was "Blackie" speaks to a lifetime of humiliation. Did the diagnosis of a "mental malady," and the prospect of life in an insane asylum, convince Sally that death was the only solution to a life not worth living?

Had the family been hiding Sally's mental condition for months, or even years, before her two suicide attempts resulted in my grandfather finally seeking medical attention? Although it is possible schizophrenia can be diagnosed as the result of just one violent episode, it is more likely that Sally had shown early signs of mental illness, but they just weren't recognized as such. In Dr. E. Fuller Torrey's comprehensive book, *Surviving Schizophrenia* (Harper Collins, 1983), he writes, "The most common early symptoms of schizophrenia as observed by the family are:

* Depression
* Changes in social behavior, especially withdrawal
* Changes in sleep or eating patterns
* Suspiciousness or feelings that people are talking about him/her
* Changes in pattern of self-care
* Changes in school performance
* Marked weakness, lack of energy
* Headaches or strange sensations in (the) head
* Changes in emotional relationships with family or close friends
* Confused, strange, or bizarre thinking"

Since virtually all information about Sally has been erased for decades, it is impossible to say whether she demonstrated any, or all, of the above-mentioned behaviors. If such actions were evident in the Levin household, it could explain why my mother agonized over her failure to safeguard her sister from harm. However, I believe that when she (my mother) insisted, "It was my job to protect her (Sally) and I didn't," what she really meant was that it was her responsibility to protect her sister from further attempts to commit suicide.

Assuming that were the case, I am completely mystified as to why my mother left for California just days before she knew Sally was to be committed to Evanston. It is even more disturbing to think my mother, Sally's closest confidant and protector, fled Cheyenne to avoid a final farewell to the sister she loved, all the while knowing her father's inevitable plan.

The state of my grandmother's mental health has long been a topic of conversation in our family. Were her odd behaviors consistent with the emotional trauma of a mother living with the tragic death of her child? Whenever I think about my grandmother, I can't help but wonder when, if ever, she was told the entire truth about how Sally died. The newspapers reported that my grandmother was in the courtroom for my grandfather's hearing and sentencing; what she understood from those legal proceedings is unclear. And, because she was illiterate, she would have been totally unaware of the countless newspaper stories related to this case.

My mother once told me that my grandmother was deathly afraid of doctors and adamantly refused to be seen by one. Thus, when I received the telephone call in my sophomore year of college that my grandmother had passed away in her sleep, having never seen a doctor even though she had complained of chest pains, I wasn't surprised.

I recall my mother also telling me that my grandmother was "not really with it most of the time" when she (my mother) was young and that it was my grandfather who did most of the housework and cared for the children. The question then is this: Was my grandmother severely depressed or suffering from some other form of undiagnosed mental illness most of her adult life? The only information I have regarding my grandmother's mental state is a recent comment made by my mother's closest childhood friend when I asked her how my grandmother handled the news of Sally's death. Her reply: "Everyone in town (Cheyenne) knew that your grandmother wasn't quite right in the head even back then."

My attempts to find out who ordered and paid for Sally's grave marker, and why her name is misspelled, have been to no avail. Perhaps a sympathetic congregant from my grandfather's synagogue donated the funds, but no such record could be found. Since the Jewish community was so small, it is unlikely that the correct spelling of Sally's name would have been unfamiliar to any such individual. It is possible that my grandfather telephoned in the grave marker order from California sometime before the one-year anniversary of Sally's death and, due to his distinct Russian accent, the individual on the other end of the line misunderstood what he said. The only other logical explanation is that the stone carver made a mistake that nobody, including my grandfather, recognized for more than seventy years. I would like to believe that had other family members ever visited the burial site, they would have noticed the error and had it corrected. I am profoundly disturbed that my mother, and members of her family, failed to tend Sally's grave site or in any way honor her memory. It is my intention to right this wrong.

The decision to keep Sally's life and death a secret lies at the very heart of this book. I wrestle with the knowledge, and the anger, that a deliberate plan was put into place to deny future generations the truth about our family history. Whether such knowledge constitutes a birthright is a matter of debate. I have spoken with many people who have shared that they too have discovered disturbing tales about their family's history that shocked them to their very core. Whether the gatekeeper of the Levin family's hidden past was my grandfather, all of his four surviving children, or a collaborative effort between them all, matters little. A family dynamic built on a foundation of secrets and shame is destined for emotional failure.

My goal in telling Sally Levin's remarkable story, at least at the outset, was to honor her memory and give voice to her life. In closing, I also wish to acknowledge my grandfather, for I believe him to be a misunderstood man in many ways. Like countless parents before him, Sam Levin was a heartbroken father with limited understanding of his child's devastating, incurable mental illness. For his deplorable actions, he must have suffered endless torment, yet he soldiered on, existing for the rest of his days on a meager diet of sorrow and regret. Although Sally was a victim of life circumstances beyond her control, it may have been inevitable that she would die an early death—either by her own hand or by another's. My grandfather's role as Sally's "mercy slayer," or as her murderer as some would choose to see it, saved his child from the suffering and disgrace she feared. For that, and for his unconditional love of me, I forgive him his horrible deed.

I search each day to better understand the events of that long-ago August morning, and all the subsequent truths that were denied me. By telling Sally's story, I hope to atone for my family's past omissions and in doing so, resurrect the memory of a young woman whose life has been lost in the debris of time.

EPILOGUE

It is my sincere hope that Sally, the girl whose life was virtually erased from memory, will live again through the pages of this book. It is my intention to replace and rededicate Sally (Sarah) Levin's grave marker to reflect both her English and Hebrew names. The following prayer will be recited over her grave.

The El Male Rachamim (God full of compassion)

אֵל מָלֵא רַחֲמִים, שׁוֹכֵן בַּמְּרוֹמִים, הַמְצֵא מְנוּחָה נְכוֹנָה עַל כַּנְפֵי הַשְּׁכִינָה, בְּמַעֲלוֹת קְדוֹשִׁים וּטְהוֹרִים כְּזֹהַר הָרָקִיעַ מַזְהִירִים, אֶת נִשְׁמַת שָׂרָה בַּת שְׁמוּאֵל שֶׁהָלְכָה לְעוֹלָמָהּ, בְּגַן עֵדֶן תְּהֵא מְנוּחָתָהּ, לָכֵן בַּעַל הָרַחֲמִים יַסְתִּירֶהָ בְּסֵתֶר כְּנָפָיו לְעוֹלָמִים, וְיִצְרוֹר בִּצְרוֹר הַחַיִּים אֶת נִשְׁמָתָהּ, יְיָ הוּא נַחֲלָתָהּ, וְתָנוּחַ בְּשָׁלוֹם עַל מִשְׁכָּבָהּ. וְנֹאמַר אָמֵן.

—Courtesy of Rabbi Richard Rheims

English translation:

O God, exalted and full of compassion, grant perfect peace in Your sheltering Presence, among the holy and pure, to the soul of Sally Levin (Sarah bat Shmuel), who has gone to her eternal home. God of mercy, protect her soul forever. May her soul be bound up in the bond of eternal life. Adonai. You are her portion. May she rest in peace. Let us say: Amen.

El Male Rachamim (God full of compassion) is a Jewish prayer for the departed that is recited at funeral services, on visiting the graves of relatives (especially during the holy month of Elul), and after having been called up to the reading of the Torah on the anniversary of the death of a close relative. The prayer originated in the Jewish communities of Western and Eastern Europe and since the end of the Holocaust, the prayer has been adapted as a memorial prayer for the victims of the Holocaust and Nazi persecution. (*Holocaust Memorial Day Trust,* http://hmd.org.uk/resources/liturgical-readings/el-male-rachamim)

SELECT BIBLIOGRAPHY

Deutsch, Albert. *The Mentally Ill in America.* 2nd ed.
New York: Columbia, 1952.

Deutsch, Albert. *The Shame of the States.*
New York: Arno Press, 1973.

Freedman, Robert. *The Madness Within Us.*
New York: Oxford University Press, 2010.

Grob, Gerald. *The Mad Among Us.*
New York: The Free Press, 1994.

Imber-Black, Evan. *The Secret Life of Families.*
New York: Bantam Books, 1998.

Kauffman, Jeffrey, editor. *The Shame of Death, Grief, and Trauma.*
New York: Routledge, 2010.

Penny, Darby and Stastny, Peter. *The Lives They Left Behind: Suitcases
From a State Hospital Attic.* New York: Bellevue Literary Press, 2009.

Saks, Elyn R. *The Center Cannot Hold*.

New York: Hyperion, 2007.

Torrey, E. Fuller. *Surviving Schizophrenia*.

New York: Harper Collins, 1983.

Torrey, E. Fuller. *The Insanity Offense*.

New York: W. W. Norton & Company, 2008.

Torrey, E. Fuller. and Judy Miller. *The Invisible Plague*.

New Jersey: Rutgers University Press, 2001.

Wolin, Penny Diane. *The Jew Of Wyoming: Fringe of the Diaspora*.

Cheyenne: Crazy Woman Creek, 2000.

Yount, Lisa. *Right to Die and Euthanasia*. Rev. ed.

New York: Infobase, 2007.